How Libraries Should Manage Data

CHANDOS
INFORMATION PROFESSIONAL SERIES
Series Editor: Ruth Rikowski
(email: Rikowskigr@aol.com)

Chandos' new series of books is aimed at the busy information professional. They have been specially commissioned to provide the reader with an authoritative view of current thinking. They are designed to provide easy-to-read and (most importantly) practical coverage of topics that are of interest to librarians and other information professionals. If you would like a full listing of current and forthcoming titles, please visit www.chandospublishing.com.

New authors: we are always pleased to receive ideas for new titles; if you would like to write a book for Chandos, please contact Dr Glyn Jones on g.jones.2@elsevier.com or telephone +44(0) 1865 843000.

How Libraries Should Manage Data

Practical Guidance on How, With Minimum Resources, to Get the Best from Your Data

Brian Cox

AMSTERDAM • BOSTON • HEIDELBERG • LONDON
NEW YORK • OXFORD • PARIS • SAN DIEGO
SAN FRANCISCO • SINGAPORE • SYDNEY • TOKYO

Chandos Publishing is an imprint of Elsevier

Chandos Publishing is an imprint of Elsevier
225 Wyman Street, Waltham, MA 02451, USA
Langford Lane, Kidlington, OX5 1GB, UK

ISBN: 978-0-08-100663-4

British Library Cataloguing-in-Publication Data
A catalogue record for this book is available from the British Library.

Library of Congress Control Number: 2015941746

For information on all Chandos Publishing
visit our website at http://store.elsevier.com/

Cover image by Brian Cox

Dedication

Dedicated to Khrystyne and Harriett

Contents

Please go to the Companion Website at http://booksite.elsevier.com/9780081006634/
to download materials mentioned in subsequent chapters, and to use these for yourself

About the author

Brian has worked in a number of different sectors, in roles that included responsibility for advocacy, privacy, copyright, records management, quality, and project management. He is currently working as Peer Learning Manager at the University of Wollongong.

Brian has been responsible for a number of activities within an academic library, ranging from managing research data collections to facilitating strategic planning. During that time Brian developed a deep understanding of how libraries use data, and where they could improve. Brian's work in this area culminated in the creation of the Library Cube, a breakthrough in measuring value that propelled the University of Wollongong Library into the international spotlight within the Library sector.

Brian has strong Excel skills, including programming in VBA, which he has used extensively to automate many otherwise labor intensive tasks, both inside and outside of the library. Brian is available to provide data management advice, and can be contacted at briancoxconsulting@outlook.com.

Introduction

1

There is a tsunami of literature on the need to demonstrate the value of libraries, and what to measure to achieve that goal. The driving force behind the production and consumption of this literature is the growing consciousness of the impact of the digital age on the library business model.

> *"Librarians have angsted for decades about what "library" might mean in the future. Their best guess is a kind of light-filled community centre offering wifi, yoga rooms, self-improvement classes and atmospheric positive thinking. The very vagueness plays into the bean-counters' hands. Nothing's easier to axe than a bunch of wishy-washy." Elizabeth Farrelly, 3 Sep 14, Sydney Morning Herald (http://www.smh.com.au/comment/library-book-dumping-signals-a-new-dark-age-20140903-10bspm.html)*

This comment was a response to the announcement that all staff at the University of Sydney Library were being made redundant, and would need to reapply for their jobs under a new staffing structure that is likely to result in some staff not being re-employed. It is a very dramatic turn of events, and something that many librarians at Sydney University probably thought would never happen.

While this is not a book about the strategic directions libraries should take, the journalist's comments do raise two issues that are absolutely critical to turning the content of this book into something useful for your library or organization. The first is that even though the journalist's comments could be written off as glib and sarcastic, and it is quite possible some librarians would find those comments offensive, they do carry a kernel of truth. There has been much angst, without much in the way of solutions.

So, if your ultimate motivation in reading this book is to uncover the "truth," to find an alternative business model, then you are putting things in the wrong order, and setting yourself up to fail.

Digging up more and more data will not provide answers. It does not matter how granular, or how detailed your data is — if you are measuring something that does not work, something that is fading, something that is becoming irrelevant — then the act of measuring more of it will not help you to find relevance. It can only tell you what you already know; your business model is broken. I cannot emphasize this enough, as many librarians are driven by an almost primal need to collect more and more data. Indeed, many librarians are data hoarders — they have a problem, and they need to remove the clutter, not add to it. And like all hoarders, they are in denial, and stress only makes things worse. Building a great wall of performance measures will not protect your organization from the hordes of technological change.

The journalist's comment also raises another point that is very pertinent to this book. If something is "wishy-washy" then throwing more measures at it will not firm things up. If you cannot describe in concrete words the value your service and/ or products are providing to clients, then there is no hope of doing so with numbers. If, for example, you wish to measure the success of a hypothetical program, say the "Collaborative and Information Technology Enriched Learning Spaces" (CITELS) program, and it turns out when all the marketing collateral is pushed aside that CITELS is simply a purple room with WIFI access and a few tables and chairs, then numbers will not help you. Sure, you could run a room bookings count, a headcount of room usage, a count of unique student usage, a sum of bandwidth usage, a breakdown of the type of internet usage, a time series of the decibels in the room, a breakdown of use by student demographic, a nonparticipant observation study of the students behavior in using CITELS... and the list could go on.

The point is that no amount of measurements will tell you anything more relevant than the room is being used – if you cannot or have not identified the value proposition of the program. The purpose of offering a service or product is to provide something of value to the client. If you are unable to clearly articulate what that value actually is, then you cannot hope to measure the value provided.

Of course, client satisfaction has long been used by libraries, what about measuring client satisfaction with CITELS? But satisfaction with what? CITELS is just a name, it is not a value proposition any more than the word "Library" defines a value proposition. If you asked the clients whether they were satisfied with CITELS using a likert scale, and 95% responded they were "Very Satisfied," then so what? It might make good marketing fodder for an uninterested or uncritical audience; however the numbers actually mean nothing. The client might be satisfied that they found a quiet place to sleep, another might think it's a great place to play computer games, another might have enjoyed catching up with friends and talking about the weekend. None of those uses are likely to correspond to the intended value proposition. Once viewed this way, it is possible to conceive that every client was "Very Satisfied" for reasons that had nothing to do with academic learning. If you don't know the intended specific value of the thing you are offering, then there is no way of knowing whether you succeeded in achieving the changes you hoped for by offering that value, and no amount of numbers will bridge that gap. I cannot underline the word "specific" enough.

The value proposition for CITELS could be many things. It might be to provide a safe space where students can work collaboratively on assignments. It might be to provide technology to enable students to work via a communication tool like skype to design and create things. These are two very different ways of using the rooms, and therefore the rooms would need to be configured quite differently to provide services to enable these uses. Similarly, the measurements you decide to adopt would need to be tailored to these differences in value propositions. Students cannot be said to be working collaboratively if they are working individually, any more than students can be said to be creating things if no objects are produced while students are in the room. It is possible to split hairs, and say what if the student started drafting something, etc. But that is completely irrelevant. Naturally you need to find the right measures, but these measures can only ever be right if they relate to the value proposition.

If you ultimately succeed in identifying appropriate measures, without really knowing why you are doing something, then you have been lucky, not clever! Once the intended benefit to the client is clearly articulated, then it should be possible to start to collect some accurate and meaningful data, not the other way around.

In summary, more data will not make "wishy-washy" value propositions come into focus, and more data on existing operations will not help you to identify new strategies to reverse the declining viability of existing business models. This book cannot help you with those specific problems. However, if you know why you are doing something, and you do not expect more numbers will magically reveal strategic opportunities, then this book might just be helpful.

What is the value proposition of this book then?

There is already a wealth of literature on what libraries should measure. I do not believe there is much value to be gained from me wading further into this field. Besides, it would only enable and encourage the data hoarders! This book is not about what to measure; it is about how to use data efficiently and effectively.

Of course, there are many books on how to measure data efficiently and effectively, these are called excel textbooks. However, as far as I am aware there is nothing targeted specifically at librarians. And on this note, librarians do need something specifically written for them.

Over the last decade I have observed what I would call a schizophrenic reaction in the library profession toward data. On one hand librarians love to collect data, but on the other hand many librarians are scared of the very things they collect. It is like an arachnophobic spider collector.

This fear of numbers is manifested in many different ways. I have witnessed librarians using a pen on a computer screen to manually count off the rows in a spreadsheet. I have seen librarians add up two cells using a calculator, then type that value manually into the cell below. I have seen librarians overwrite formulas with values, to force two sheets to reconcile. These are intelligent people doing dumb things, because they are scared of excel — and they are frequently scared of excel because they are scared of numbers. This fear cannot be overcome with excel textbooks, as they are designed for an audience that is numerically confident and literate. Also, being quite detailed focused; I have frequently found librarians tend to be literal, which means many can struggle to apply external concepts to the library profession. This of course is a generalization, and a generalization that does not discuss many of the wonderful attributes of a typical librarian. So, if you are feeling a bit offended, please don't. The profession is full of wonderful people, and I would much rather a librarian any day over an engineer! You have picked up this book for a reason, and by logical deduction it means you need help with data. So let's accept you have some issues to work through with data, and get on with it!

Lifting the fog

2

Imagine your house is in shambles, clothes piled up in random containers tucked away in dark corners, shoe boxes collecting dust balancing precariously on the top of wardrobes, and you are sick of the state of mess. There is a sensible way to go about cleaning, and an irrational way. It is quite possible that the reason you have a mess is because you have more than you need. That dress may have looked great on you in your early twenties, but it is never going to fit again. And those pair of shoes you wore to your first job have gone out of style along with other relics that should stay in the past, like mullet haircuts. So, if you are serious about cleaning, this means letting go of some things. Easy said, not so easy to do.

The same applies to data. You might have some wonderful time series data that makes a pretty chart, or you might have some stats that staff have been collecting since the Stone Age, or you might have some statistics to which staff feel emotionally attached. Just because you collected it in the past does not mean you should have ever collected it, or even if it once was a legitimate collection from a business perspective, it does not mean that it is now. Just like the messy house, a bloated collection of irrelevant data, is counterproductive. At the very best irrelevance distracts from the data that is useful. At worst, the good data gets tainted by the bad data, with staff becoming cynical or disconnected with data. If the numerical literacy at your workplace is low, then chances are this will provide comfortable validation for those staff that want nothing to do with numbers.

When you are cleaning your house, the last thing you should do is rush off and buy more storage, and perhaps buy more clothes and shoes. This would only make the mess worse. The same applies to data. If you are not happy with the state of affairs with your data, don't rush off and create new spreadsheets, sign up to new data vendors, or collect more data. Useful things become useless if they are hidden in a sea of rubbish. Indeed, this is meant to be one of the key value propositions of the library — they are a gateway to quality resources. Unfortunately, many professions don't practice what they preach. However, if you are worried about the long term viability of your business model, then you will need good data; and to get good data you need to be disciplined and focused.

What is the first sensible thing to do when cleaning your house? You decide on criteria for determining whether to keep something or not, then assess whether the things you have meet those criteria. You would at the very least have three piles, one pile for stuff to keep, one to give away, another to chuck. Your criteria might be simple — it might be I will keep it if it fits me, and I will allow myself to keep five items for sentimental value.

When you are cleaning your data it is essential that you determine the criteria before you start. Cleaning data can be an emotional exercise, and if you don't determine the criteria first, chances are you will inadvertently allow emotion to make the decisions. Of course, emotions for data are quite different to clothes. The emotional response might be something like:

1. I really don't know why we ever collected this, but what happens if I chuck it and we need it later
2. I don't understand this data, and I don't want to admit that, so let's just hang onto it
3. No one understands what we do, and if we don't collect that data people will think we are not important, or not busy
4. I don't know what I need to collect because I have no idea how to use the data, so let's just keep collecting as much as possible and hope that the avalanche of statistics will somehow morph into something useful
5. It is all too hard, it is easier just to keep collecting it, besides, it does not take that long

None of the above are sound business reasons for keeping data, and therefore if you allow these types of reasons to unconsciously determine your choices, then chances are you will dispose of nothing. Now, if you have been lucky, and all your data is good data, then well done, go and buy a lottery ticket while the gods are smiling on you. However, chances are you have some bad data, which means anything you do to try to improve the good data will deliver slim value.

You might be asking what do you mean by good data. The sole purpose of data is to prove a point to an unconvinced audience, or help you to make a decision. If your stakeholders are worried about the value your library is delivering to clients, then you will need data to help put their minds at ease. If you want to create a new service, but are not sure whether there is the demand for such a service, then you need data to help identify the business case. Good data allows an organization to thrive, it can be used to build strong positive perceptions about your library, it can be used to drive continuous improvement, and occasionally it can be used to assess business cases for new ventures. Bad data is the fog that obscures the use-value of good data.

So what sort of criteria should you use to help you with your data de-cluttering? Broadly speaking, you should be collecting data to answer one of four questions:

1. How much **effort** am I putting into producing a given service/product
2. What is the **demand** for services/products I am producing
3. What is the perceived **value** of my efforts to clients
4. What is the **outcome** of my efforts for clients

If your data does not answer any of the above questions, or answers them very poorly, then why keep collecting this data? The only possible valid answer is because you are required to collect that specific dataset by law. There are peak bodies that require the collection of statistics that are not of much use locally. The question you will need to answer is whether the cost of providing that data to the peak body is worth the goodwill. Here the cost is not just the time spent collecting and reporting on the data, but the contribution it makes to the fog of irrelevant information.

Some people may think these four questions are arbitrary, and certainly they are from the perspective of the terminology I used. There are a lot of key performance indicators out there, and a lot of tools for organizing them, such as the balanced scorecard. But focusing too much on the terminology at this stage runs the real risk of driving the data renewal program irretrievably into a semantic bog.

When I first started facilitating planning sessions at an academic library, I was amazed by how much energy staff were putting into crafting the right words for strategic goals. Eventually, I became a bit tired of the exercise and said quite loudly, "stop polishing stones." My strange statement stunned a few people into silence, and when everyone turned to look at me I continued:

> *Your strength is also your weakness. Everyone here is great at crafting sentences, they are like finely polished stones. But before we start polishing stones we need to make sure that we have the right stones to begin with. If you have chosen the wrong course of action for the library's strategic direction, then no amount of word smithing is going to help. In fact, it will hinder progress, because you will have these bright shiny stones that no one is going to want to let go of.*

The same logic applies to your criteria. Focus on choosing the right criteria first, not crafting words first. The meaning of course needs to be clear, but you are not writing the constitution for a newly formed nation state. Lofty words and lengthy criteria will make the de-cluttering exercise more difficult, and wherever difficulty exists, emotion can sneak into the decision making process.

On the subject of decision making, one of the first things you will need to do before you starting de-cluttering is to identify who is authorized to make the decisions. One option is to do the following:

- If the data is never used outside the team, then the team leader takes authority for disposal
- If the data is never used outside the division, then the division manager makes the decision
- All other decisions are made by the Director/Librarian

This is a nice way to devolve responsibility; however, if you have a strong culture of data hoarding, then some people are quite likely to make emotional decisions with their data, despite your best efforts at communicating the criteria. In this situation a simple audit of everything might be required, with more central decision making. Otherwise, you risk going through a big exercise without culling much, which only risks further spreading the perception that data is irrelevant. Consequently, the best approach is to manage your data culling exercise as a project.

Projects have been around for a very long time, and there are many fine books written on the subject. There is a strong body of knowledge and scholarship on the principles of good project management, principles that have been refined over the centuries. As this is meant to be a practical handbook, and not an academic text, I am not going to discuss theory of project management, only what you need to consider in the library context for this specific project.

First steps — project management

Some libraries can struggle a bit with projects, so managing the change with a tool with dubious success might seem to some like saddling up for double barrelled failure. It does not have to be that way. If people struggle with projects, then don't call it a project. But make sure you run it like one. Briefly, you need a project when you are doing something for the first time, and you require the coordination of several people, people that are dispersed across several teams.

If you are doing something for the first time, then you cannot use existing policy or procedures to manage the work. So you have two options. Make it up as you go along, with frequent team meetings to give the illusion of organization. This option is the no-win option. If you succeed, then it is down to luck — and if you fail, then it is your fault for not managing the thing properly. The other option is to plan what you are going to do before you start doing something. If you do this, then odds on you will be managing it as a project.

If you agree that the first step to improving the usefulness of your data is to de-clutter, and you agree that you need to adopt a project management approach to doing this, then the VERY first step you need to take is to ensure that you have full executive support. If you are the Director, then wonderful; if you have read this far chances are you are committed to changing data management. If you are not the Director, then you will need to ensure that you can sell the benefit of doing this to the executive.

A lot of people don't like changing things they think are working, and if you attempt this project with only half-baked executive support, then at the first sign of any hardship, staff will default to saying they are too busy to help. The message needs to be clear with the executive team marching in locked step — we are going to improve our data management, here is the reason why, here is what we will do, here is when it will be done, and here is who is responsible. If you have that level of executive support, then you are well on your way to success.

Before you start communications, you need to sit down with the executive to obtain clear and realistic expectations on what you hope to achieve, and what sort of resourcing the project will need. Once everyone has agreed to this, you need to document this agreement, then identify a project sponsor and a project manager. These two roles can be confused a bit, so the following analogy might help.

Imagine you have just bought a wonderful block of land. It has great ocean views, and a lot of potential for gardening, which incidentally you happen to love! The land is empty, and you want to build your dream house on it. Imagine you have a rough vision for what you want your house to look like, but you don't have the expertise, knowledge, and/or experience to translate that vision into an actual house. So you need to contract an architect and builder to do this for you. Now, unless you are very naive, or have some good reason to leave the architect and builder alone to their own devices, chances are you will want to catch up at certain stages to make sure everything is going along well. It's your house, and you don't want to run the risk of ending up with something awful at the end of it, when it is all too late. On the other hand, you are not a builder or an architect, so if you start attempting to manage the project as if you were a builder or an architect, then chances are you will only cause bottlenecks and miscommunications. This can only result in cost blow outs, delays, and poorer quality of work.

A project sponsor is like the home owner. They have a vested interest in ensuring the project is finished on time, on budget, and to specification. So, they manage this vested interest by checking in occasionally with the project manager. They might do this at certain predetermined milestones, or on a monthly basis. However, this checking in is not about managing the project.

A sponsor that takes over the project management is about as useful as a manager that does the job of their staff. If you are a project sponsor, and you do tend to micromanage, then be aware of it and have strategies to deal with it. If you cannot help yourself, get someone else to be the sponsor. Occasionally there will be roadblocks that are too big for the project manager to navigate by themselves. In these instances they may need to have the project sponsor weigh in, and throw their support behind the project. However, this should be a last resort, not the modus operandi of the project.

The same logic applies to the project manager. The project manager will have a team of people that will take responsibility for completing specific tasks by a due date to a specific standard. If the project manager starts micromanaging their team, then they will end up creating bottlenecks, delays, and by taking away responsibility from their team, it is likely that the quality of the team's work will decline. When you hand a task to someone, it then becomes their responsibility to get that task done, and if they cannot, it is their responsibility to communicate any problems to the project manager as soon as possible.

When you have identified who will be the project manager, and who will be the project sponsor, then the project manager will need to draft up a project plan, and get sign off on the plan from the project sponsor. The project plan needs to identify what you are aiming to achieve. This will be the deliverable. If you were building a house, and you commissioned an architect to design a house, without any further input, then it is highly unlikely that you will end up with a design that remotely resembles anything you hoped for. The same applies to this project. If you are vague about what you hope to achieve, i.e., the deliverables are not clearly specified, then chances are no one is going to be satisfied with the project upon completion. This cannot be empathized enough. The deliverables for a project specify exactly what you hope to deliver at the end of the project — don't assume everyone shares the same vision, because they will not. A clear and specific set of project deliverables will keep the project manager accountable and focused, and will ensure that the scope of the project stays contained.

This second point is also very important, because Librarians can tend to be perfectionists. If you try do to everything perfectly, then the scope of the project will grow and grow, to the point where it becomes so big it is impossible to complete. Everyone has their own vested interests, their own priorities, and their own view on how things should be done. All these things can and will place pressure on the project. There will be some pressure to reshape the project, some pressure from other corners to reduce its scope, and most likely, much pressure from many areas to expand its scope. This is so common it has a name, scope creep. As project manager you have to manage expectations tightly, both at the beginning and throughout the lifecycle of the project.

Once the project plan has received executive support, the next step is for the project manager to get the team together, to introduce them to the plan, each other, and their roles. Depending on the project team, you might wish to get them more involved in fleshing out the details of the plan, and identifying any gaps. If you have a small library, then the whole project could be left to one person. However, even if it is only a team of one, you still need to document what is expected from you, and plan ahead. Otherwise you are just making things up as you go along and therefore leaving success to chance.

I have witnessed many projects where it was not clear why something was being done. In the absence of information, staff make up their own minds. This can be dangerous, as it can lead to misinformed views which create real roadblocks. For example, at one place I worked, management decided to run an Activity Based Costing exercise, and did not do a very good job communicating why. This resulted in a lot of defensive posturing from some staff, with the result that the data quality was probably nowhere near as high as could have otherwise been achieved.

Library staff tend to be older, they have witnessed and been involved in many changes. Many are skeptical and cynical about change, particularly when you frequently see changes that after a decade end up coming round full circle. So it is absolutely imperative that the Director makes it very clear to all staff at the start of the project why they have commissioned this project. The Director needs to provide a compelling case for change. For example, a more theatrical Director might say something like this:

Over the past decades there have been many changes that have had a great impact on libraries. Even though we have embraced digital technologies, our fundamental business model has remained in large parts unchanged for centuries. The value we provided in the past does not guarantee that we will continue to provide value in the future. We are at the moment largely adrift on the sea of technological change. We have adopted technologies to our existing business model as these technologies have emerged. We have let go of some services, and created new ones. But we have for the large part been consigned to the role of reacting to change. If the tide and wind were with us, then we could have the option of continuing to drift. But it is not. We need to focus on and grow the new services that meet new demands. But we cannot strike out in the right direction when we are surrounded by fog. Data can tell us where we have been successful, and it can tell us where we can improve. Data can also tell us changes in trends, and potential new directions we could take. The problem is we are collecting so much data that does not need to be collected; and the data that is relevant, is out of date, inaccurate, and/or is too difficult to obtain in a timely manner. This is our fog. We are adrift in a data fog. For our long term success, we have to lift this fog. If we can clear the data fog we will be better able to determine whether we have been successful in our effort to reach new shores, and we will be better placed to know what we need to change when we drift off course.

With this in mind, I have asked Josephine Bloggs to review the data we are collecting, make recommendations on what we need to let go of, what we need to improve, and what new information we need to collect. That's stage one of the project. The second stage is to recommend and implement new ways of managing this data. This is an important project. This project must succeed. I am sure you will give Josephine your full support. She will be forming a project team shortly, and will keep us informed of updates on the staff intranet.

I do not believe for a moment that any Library Director on this planet would give such a speech. I have worded it this way partly for some light hearted entertainment. But I also used the unlikely words of a Library Director as a device to draw sharp attention to a theme that underlies much of this book, the importance of using data to be good. This theme will be more fully explored as you progress through this book.

Now, while I am in full analogy swing, I would like to reiterate that data is not magical. It will not tell you exactly were to head. Most data is lagging. It tells you how things were. The Vikings used to trail rope behind their boats to tell if they were going in a straight line. The rope would tell them if they had shifted course recently, but it certainly would not help them to identify if their course was heading in the right direction. It only told them if they had stuck to their chosen course. Much of your operational data is like that rope.

After you have convinced staff of the need for change, the first task of de-cluttering then becomes a relatively simple one of auditing all the data being collecting by the organization, and assessing the value of the data against the prede-termined selection criteria. This will need to be done in conjunction with the data owners. The person making the assessment might come to a different opinion on the value of the data being collected, but that difference should be informed by the application of the selection criteria, rather than ignorance of what, how and why the data is being collected. I suggest you start first with a friend, hone your technique and tools, before consulting more widely within the library.

The purpose of the audit should be to collect enough information to help you make informed decisions about which datasets to delete, improve, change or add. Once you have finished the audit process, you need to write up recommendations for your Library Director. Depending upon the complexity of the situation, some further consultation may be required before making a decision on a particular data-set. Before you get to this point, you will also need to think about how you are going to go about telling someone that their data will no longer be collected, or will be substantially changed. Stick to the facts, be friendly and respectful, but keep it away from the personal level. Try to think of a way of phrasing constructive feed-back beforehand, for example:

As you know I have been reviewing the data being collected by the Library. I have reviewed a few datasets with you, and I greatly appreciate your help. We could see that the data was definitely useful in the past, and has been included in

*management reports many times. After careful consideration we think we probably
do not need to collect this data from this point forward. There is however, other
data that we will need from your team, and I will definitely need your advice and
help with this at a later point. Meanwhile, how do we go about decommissioning
this dataset?*

Some staff may be happy to let go of the data, but others might take it a bit personally, particularly if they have been collecting it for years, and perceive it to be
more valuable than it actually is. Just imagine someone with authority in your
library told you that everything you were doing was rubbish. Well, obviously in
this case it's not everything, but you will get the idea. Telling staff they need to
stop something could potentially be quite hurtful, so you will just need to be mind-
ful of this to avoid unnecessarily bruising egos.

You will also need to consider who to consult in decommissioning data. It will
probably be the team leaders, but you should have sorted this out as part of your
earlier recommendations to the Director.

At the end of this process you should have a list that contains:

- All significant datasets collected by your library
- A very brief description of each dataset, including how it is currently used
- The location of the dataset
- Who owns each dataset
- A very brief assessment of how each dataset meets the data assessment criteria. For exam-
  ple, how well does it currently answer any of the questions below:
  - How much **effort** am I putting into producing a given service/product
  - What is the **demand** for services/products I am producing
  - What is the perceived **value** of my efforts to clients
  - What is the **outcome** of my efforts for clients
- Brief comments on how the datasets' use-value could be improved

Once you have collected this information, you will be ready to discuss the findings with the Director and Project Sponsor. This is a very critical stage, and the success of the data re-invigoration project will hang off how willing management is to
make hard decisions, and stick to them.

Once you have your slimmer data, you will be ready to reshape the management
of your data, so that information can be easily, reliably, and accurately retrieved.
Before you can do that, however, you need to identify the best way to organize
your data. The following chapters will show you how.

Step away from the spreadsheet – common errors in using spreadsheets, and their ramifications

3

How Libraries Should Manage Data.

A while back I was talking to a librarian who was having problems with the pivot tables I created. She insisted that the pivots were calculating incorrectly because it was showing that $13 + 4 = 17$, when it should show 16. I told her jokingly, like a police officer would, that she needed to step away from the spreadsheet. Once the penny dropped for her we both laughed about it, and in this instance it was just one of those silly mistakes that we all make from time to time. Excel, however, can be problematic – and if someone is not data literate, they can use Excel to create many headaches.

Excel is incredibly powerful. Very few people understand its true power; and just like a high powered muscle car can be devastating in the hands of a learner, so to can Excel become a problem if it is not driven correctly.

It is possible to use Excel as a tool to interrogate webpages, email, word documents, and open, change, and delete files. I know as I have written many programs using Excel VBA to do many things, such as webscraping, timetabling, conducting fuzzy matches, and writing complex algorithms to automate processes. Excel is much more than just a battery of cells into which you plug numbers and formulas. Excel also has many addins – such as PowerQuery and PowerPivot, that take the functionality of Excel to a completely new plane. PowerPivot can be used to manipulate huge datasets, and its functionality, from the point of view of the likely library needs, brings it very close to that provided by data warehousing tools.

Most people who use Excel are only skating on a very thin surface of its true functionality, happily oblivious to the vast wealth of possibilities beneath them. Now, you do not need to become an Excel guru to manage your data more effectively. You may continue to be happily oblivious to its full power. You do, however, need to change the way you think about data. But this is not a big change. It is not like asking you to understand how time and space is relative, or conceive of more than three physical dimensions. If you can read, then you can with a small amount of discipline, and an open mind, change the way you view data so as that you are able to manage it much more effectively.

I have frequently found that when people see a lot of blank cells, and the option of adding an endless number of additional sheets, the first thing they do is treat Excel like a big sprawling canvas, onto which they can paint their data in the way that suits their individual tastes and needs. And every painting seems to be different, regardless of who paints it, or how many they have painted before. Each one is a special artwork, requiring art critics to help you to interpret the painting. This has to stop. The reason it needs to stop is also the same reason why almost all users default to using Excel as an art canvas.

Almost all library staff seem to have three considerations in mind when creating a new spreadsheet: I want to do this quickly, I want to make it easy for staff to enter data, and it needs to be easy for me to report on the data. By itself, this is a reasonable set of criteria. However, in practice, because staff tend to think of Excel in the same way they conceive tables in a Word document, they produce the least optimal data structures conceivable.

Library staff, and indeed most other staff I have worked with, first and only response when having to create a new spreadsheet is to enter their data into crosstab tables. For example, if staff needed to collect data on browsed items (items that clients have removed from the shelves, but not borrowed), then staff might typically create a spreadsheet that contains date in the columns (vertical), with the library location in the rows (horizontal). They might even have more granular data into the row header, specifying which location in the library the book was browsed.

Browsed items, 2015

Date	Main Library			X Library		Y Library	Total
	1st Floor	2nd Floor	3rd Floor	1st Floor	2nd Floor	1st Floor	
1-Jan-15	174	105	309	58	168	99	913
2-Jan-15	175	270	236	70	266	85	1102
3-Jan-15	82	216	225	92	119	62	796
4-Jan-15	81	236	283	59	195	100	954
5-Jan-15	198	162	298	79	144	73	954
6-Jan-15	157	221	374	58	143	64	1017
7-Jan-15	117	294	383	83	194	73	1144
8-Jan-15	169	152	242	68	123	95	849
9-Jan-15	51	122	301	75	239	95	883
10-Jan-15	112	271	357	87	214	73	1114
11-Jan-15	148	268	282	63	248	88	1097
12-Jan-15	104	171	247	88	194	61	865
13-Jan-15	85	280	231	93	208	64	961
14-Jan-15	108	179	238	77	124	71	797
15-Jan-15	92	135	203	95	183	66	774
16-Jan-15	127	152	300	98	257	90	1024
17-Jan-15	103	134	265	92	210	61	865
18-Jan-15	106	152	397	89	211	54	1009
19-Jan-15	61	266	400	83	145	97	1052
20-Jan-15	111	184	312	68	133	79	887
21-Jan-15	118	103	238	59	114	85	717
22-Jan-15	192	146	315	80	255	84	1072
23-Jan-15	85	104	343	52	122	65	771
24-Jan-15	71	182	329	91	282	80	1035
25-Jan-15	175	172	393	97	271	89	1197
26-Jan-15	150	111	378	89	272	72	1072
27-Jan-15	154	148	234	92	206	78	912
28-Jan-15	195	108	233	60	228	66	890
29-Jan-15	180	218	330	59	285	84	1156
30-Jan-15	57	222	242	97	110	98	826
31-Jan-15	182	236	362	89	185	99	1153
Total	3920	5720	9280	2440	6048	2450	29858

The staff that are entering the data love this structure, because once they are familiar with it, there is minimal data entry, it is easy to see where to put the data, and it is easy to see what data you have already entered. And because librarians tend to love collecting data, they tend to find this exercise satisfying. Data is only rarely reported on, and when it is, it tends to be on the bottom line figure.

Because the spreadsheet creator tends to be focused mostly on making data entry simpler, and because they tend to think of Excel the way someone might look at a table in a word document, they attempt to organize the data as best they can so as that the whole table is visible on the one screen. This typically means a new tab is created for each month, and perhaps a total tab at the end that sums up all the months. Typically, an entirely new spreadsheet would be created for each year.

The problem with this approach is that too much energy has been focused on making it easy to put data into the bucket, at the expense of getting the data out of the bucket. This structure only enables you to easily retrieve the most simple of data views. Yet, so many staff in my experience place 99% of their energies into making it easy to put the data in the bucket. I have said to so many staff, if you are never going to retrieve the data from the bucket, then why put it in there in the first place? You might as well spend a truckload of energy creating something, and then throw it in a black hole.

Rule number one should always be: most of your energy should be spent on making it easy to get the data out of the bucket. If the data cannot be used, the whole exercise will be a giant waste of time, no matter how easy you made the data entry.

Lets say management noticed a lot more clients in the library over the last few years, but noted that loans were declining over the same period. There was some pressure to free the space used by the stacks to create group study spaces. However, being a library, they did not want to reduce the stacks, unless absolutely necessary. So management wanted to know if students were browsing instead of borrowing, and they wanted to know how this was trending over the last 7 years. To answer this question, a staff member would need to open each of the seven spreadsheets, and copy the number from the totals tab, then paste that number as a value into a new spreadsheet. Now, lets say you did this, then gave the data to management and they went, OK, browsing has been declining overall in line with loans, but has this been the case for every one of our locations — and what is the ratio between loans and browsing at each location? So now you have to go back to the spreadsheet, open seven browsing spreadsheets, copy the total for each location into a new spreadsheet, do the same with loans, then create formulas for the ratios. This is going to take you at least an hour — because there is so much manual copying and pasting, you want to be sure that you have got it right, so you triple check all the figures.

Then you go back to management, they look at the data, and say, well it looks like we could clear some stacks at this location, but which level is being used the most? To answer this question you are going to have to open up all seven spreadsheets again, and then add formulas to them, because the totals formulas at the end of the spreadsheet only captured totals for each location, not the totals for the levels. You have to completely rebuild the totals tabs on all seven spreadsheets, double check that they are summing correctly, copy the values from the seven spreadsheets, and paste all those values into a new spreadsheet. This is likely to take 2—3 hours.

These are very simple questions being asked of the browsed data, and they should be able to be answered within 5 min. If anything more sophisticated was asked, such as a correlation between loans and browsed items to help model and forecast demand, then the data from all seven spreadsheets will need to be radically restructured, and this is likely to take a week. Once again, this is a question your spreadsheet should be able to answer in 5 min.

So instead of being useful from a business point of view, the spreadsheets are aesthetically beautiful. They are beautiful because only a select few of the chosen special people can interpret them, they are beautiful because they are unique, one off hand crafted masterpieces, complete with the full array of gaudy colors available to the Excel artists. These spreadsheet provide a wonderful data entry experience too, and they make the users feel all warm and fuzzy. Look how busy we are. As special as these artworks are, however,they need to be taken off the wall, and put somewhere that they will never be used again.

To succeed in standardizing your spreadsheets into a useful data structure, you will need to control who is allowed to create new spreadsheets, and specify which spreadsheets are to be used for which purpose. This may sound draconian, but your choices are simple. Allow users to handcraft artworks that will only ever be useful for the most simplistic purposes, or control the creation and use of spreadsheets centrally. If you want to take control of your business' destiny, then you only have one option; centralized data management. This, of course, requires full executive support, and many staff are quite possessive of their spreadsheets, and may be reluctant to relinquish control, or to have them changed significantly.

Consequently, depending upon the size of your institution, and the complexity of the change, you may need to conduct some formal training when you roll out the new spreadsheets. Once again, the very first thing you should emphasize at the training, even if they have heard it a million times before, is why you are doing this, and what you expect to achieve. People are much more likely to come on board with you if they understand the reason for change, even if they do not agree with you.

The training issue can be taken too far though. For example, one of the first spreadsheets I started to restructure when I was running my project was the visits spreadsheets. This was and is an important statistic, as it helps the library to make informed decisions about things such as rosters and the timing of promotions. These spreadsheets, like all the others, were a complete mess. The gate counter statistics for the last 7 years were contained in about half a dozen spreadsheets spread over just as many tabs with each tab containing a different structure of data with up to 18 columns. I took this big bowl of spaghetti, and transformed it into a single spreadsheet, with one raw data tab containing four columns: Date, Location, Time, and Visits. I assumed I had made things simpler. Yet after I made these changes I had one librarian make an angry phone call to me to say there have been all these changes to the gate statistics spreadsheets, and demanded training. It was not one of my better days, so my response was not my finest hour. I told her that the old spreadsheets were almost indecipherable, and the new one only contains four columns, and even though it is blindingly obvious how to use them, nevertheless I would be happy to provide her with the training right now over the phone. I said the first column is Date, that's the date the visits were made on, and it is calculated as the number of days since Christ was born, using a calendar that evolved from Roman days. I then said the next column is Location, and unless aliens had visited earth and teleported your library to a new place, then your library will always be at the same location, so you will always enter the same thing for that column. I said the time is the thing you will find on your watch. Finally, I said the number of visits is the number of people who have entered your library on that particular day, and you read this off the gate counter the same way as you have always read it off the counter — the only difference is you now put it in a different spreadsheet. I said your training is now complete, a certificate will be in the mail shortly, and hung up.

Obviously, this was a terrible thing to say for many reasons, and it did come back to bite me quite a few times. Don't suffer fools, but make sure you do it in a productive way. It can be frustrating at times, particularly if you are trying to make sensible improvements in an environment that is resistive to change. You need to expect it will be frustrating occasionally, and manage yourself accordingly.

The new visits spreadsheet was resisted, because of two reasons. One it involved change, a change that made data more visible. This now meant anyone could with a couple of clicks see data on visits, without requiring some complex road map. There will always be a minority of staff that relish control, and they will not like the loss of control that these changes bring. The second reason is many people value the time they spend entering the data, but do not grasp the value that data could provide. So to these people such changes appear wasteful.

The ten table commandments

Getting your table structure correct is very important, and this is addressed in the next chapter. There are some other classic problems that you need to recognize as problems, before you start building something new. After all, you are reading this because you want to break the cycle of spreadsheets creating work for you; instead of them saving you work. So below is a list of things that you should absolutely *not* do.

One — Don't spread your spreadsheets around directories like confetti. Don't spread the love! Staff should not need a road map to find statistics. If it is tucked away ten layers deep in a team folder, then finding it might be obvious to those that regularly use it, but to others it might as well be a mythical unicorn! Put all your spreadsheets your staff are using in one place, and if you are no longer using a spreadsheet, then archive it off somewhere, but that should be one place too.

Two — Do not use different structures for spreadsheets. Most spreadsheets will only require three visible sheets: a raw data sheet into which all the raw data is placed, a set of pivot tables, and a contents page linking users to those pivots. You should stick with these same three sheets, and use the same name and layout for all your workbooks. If your raw data headers start in row 10 in one workbook, then there is absolutely no reason why they should not start in row 10 for all workbooks. If your raw data sheet is called "RawData" in one workbook, then don't call it something different in the next workbook. If you are going to use conditional highlighting to color code locations, then use the same color coding for all spreadsheets that contain the location field. Wherever you can be consistent, be consistent. Consistency makes it easier to maintain, and easier for staff to use. This last point is critical. If some of your staff are scared of Excel, then you will be making their life a lot easier. Once they learn how to use one of your spreadsheets, they will soon be able to use any of your spreadsheets.

Three — Do not use trendy, vague or vain names for spreadsheets. Try to base the name on what is being measured, not the team doing the activity, or even the name of the service. Many organizations put their teams through a revolving door of name changes, both for teams and their services. What is called the "Refuse Solutions Team" this week, might simply be called the cleaning team next week. So, if the spreadsheet is a cleaning roster, then call it that, not something soon to become indecipherable like "Refuse Solutions Team Future Work Scheduling Matrix.xlsx". A reasonably intelligent staff member should be able to look at the name of your spreadsheet in 5 years' time, and still know what to roughly expect without having to earnestly furrow their brows in thoughtful contemplation before opening the spreadsheet.

Four — Do not leave your spreadsheets unprotected. Many users are unconscious Excel vandals. If you give them the chance they will delete your formulas, move data, create new sheets, write new formulas (often incorrectly), change your headers, change old data, and generally wreak havoc. Chapter 6 will cover how to do this properly.

Five — Do not show users irrelevant data. Your users will not need to see many of the formulas in your raw data sheet. You might feel they make you look smart, but they will only annoy, or worse, confuse your users. If the user does not need to see the columns, hide them. If the user does not need to see a sheet (e.g., the data validation sheet), then hide the whole sheet. This will reduce the complexity of your workbook, making it easier to use, and this ease of use will help improve data integrity. For example, your staff will be less likely to procrastinate over entering their data for months on end. This leads to the next commandment. . .

Six — Do not leave data entry unmanaged. If users are left to their own devices, they will enter data whenever they feel like it. This might mean today they add an information literacy class they ran 2 years ago to the spreadsheet. The problem with this is when you run the report now for the number of information literacy classes taught over the last 3 years, the numbers you get for those years will not be the same as the report you ran last year. It is very embarrassing having to go to the Director to explain why the numbers you provided for previous annual reports have to be changed in the current annual report. Depending upon your Director you might receive a response ranging from rage to a resigned nod! This can all be avoided. Every quarter I lock down the statistics. This means I do two things. Firstly I lock all the cells for everything except the current quarter. That means no one can go back and retrospectively fiddle with numbers. The second thing I do is change the data validation rules, so as that no one can enter a date prior to the current quarter. That way staff cannot do something like add an information literacy class from 2 years ago.

At first quite a few staff responded negatively to this new approach. They were used to being able to update the data as they saw fit, and they did not enjoy the more regimental approach. They would say to me after the lock-down period closed, often months after, that "I forgot to add this, can you please add it now." Most times my answer would be a respectful "no." They of course responded that the data would be inaccurate, to which I would agree. I would say, however, that if I allow staff to add data whenever they wish, then the data we report on in important documents, such as our annual report, will be even more inaccurate, because it will always be missing significant amounts of data that staff have not been required to enter. The few inaccuracies we get from people missing lockdowns are considerably less than the inaccuracies we would get without the lockdowns. I would then add that I know this is a harsh approach, but I am sure that staff will become more proactive in future about entering data before the lockdowns. And this is precisely what happened. Staff became used to the data lockdowns, and made sure they updated their data in time. If you want your annual report, or business plan progress reports, or any other reports to accurately reflect what you have done during a period, then you will simply have to be ruthless about enforcing lockdowns. The truth is, you are only asking for a modicum of discipline, and those staff that miss the first couple of lockdowns will soon get the picture. It is absolutely wonderful to be able to run statistical reports for a given period, and still get exactly the same number for that period 5 years later, and be confident that the data is accurate. This is how it should be, and how it can be.

Seven — Do not allow users to type whatever they feel like into cells. You will need to apply data validation rules to your spreadsheets for quality assurance reasons. Data validation means the user cannot type whatever they feel like in a cell, they have to enter a specific value from a list, enter a number within a range, or enter a date. Chapter 6 will cover how to use data validation.

Eight — Do not put your lookup tables in the raw data sheet. Store your lookup tables and validations lists in a new worksheet and call it "Validation." If you don't know what lookup tables are now, you will by then end of the next chapter.

There are many reasons why you would want to store your lookups and validation lists separately, and this will become more compelling as you progress through this book. Firstly, having the lookup table on the rawdata screen only adds clutter. 99.9% of the time, the only people looking at the raw data worksheet will be the staff doing the data entry. The clutter will not help them to do their job more accurately and efficiently. The second reason for putting the lookups on a different worksheet is because if you extend the number of columns in your raw data, then depending upon where you put your lookup table you may find yourself running out of real estate. You can always move the lookup table, but why double handle when you can put it out of the way for good in the first place. Thirdly, on some rare occasions, you may need to delete rows of data. This can be done without interfering with existing tables, but it is safer not to have your lookups occupying the same rows as your raw data in the first place. Finally, it makes it easier to edit the list. If you have tens of thousands of rows of raw data, you may have to unhide some rows and columns, and then change the freeze panes settings to be able to edit your lookup tables. If your lookups are on a different sheet to your raw data this will never be a problem.

Nine — Never ask a user to enter a value that can be automatically generated via a formula. If you can write a formula to do something, then write the formula. Not only will this improve data entry speed, but it will also make your data accurate. Whenever someone enters something into a spreadsheet, there is a chance they will enter it incorrectly. You need to design spreadsheets to minimize this risk, and one of the first steps to minimizing this risk is to use formulas wherever possible.

Ten — Make people responsible for their own mess. If staff refuse to stop creating their own spreadsheets, then make them responsible for reporting, demand that they be able to do it to the depth and speed that you will be able to with your standard spreadsheets, and ensure they wear full responsibility for data loss and other inaccuracies that will inevitably occur with poorly designed spreadsheets used by multiple staff. There are not many staff that would be willing to saddle up for that responsibility, and if they are, wonderful, its no longer your problem — its theirs!

Starting from scratch

4

There are two basic steps to creating data that can be sliced and diced very easily, and to a high level of granularity. The first step is to organize the data into a single table, in a certain structure. The second step is to run a pivot table over the data. Chances are you are not very familiar with pivots, so I have devoted Chapter 7 to them. For the moment you will just have to take it on faith when I say that they make life infinitely easier. The first step, organizing your data into a single table is by far the most difficult step. However, the catch is it can appear to be the easiest step.

The first step to creating a raw data table is to understand the data you are collecting. A good way to do this is to start at the very beginning, the point at which the data is first created. Try to conceptualize the data as a series of events, to which you can assign attributes. For example, if someone comes in to borrow a book, then that book being borrowed is a single event. From a practical point of view, it is not possible to break this down any further. The borrower might come toward the lending desk or machine, and change their mind. They might get the desk and find they cannot borrow as they have already borrowed the maximum number of loans. For any event, it is always theoretically possible to break the event down further. However, from a practical point of view, there is a point beyond which it would be silly to attempt further subdivision of an event. In this example, the "sensible" point to stop, the most granular level that we care about, is at the act of borrowing a specific item.

If the book is borrowed, then there are a whole heap of other things that can be attributed to that event. The event happens at a specific time, at a specific place, the book is borrowed by a specific client for a period, the borrower has attributes — such as their gender and age, the book has attributes — such as its authors and year of publication, the library has attributes — such as the size of its collection and its opening hours. And the list could go on and on. An event is both caused by and causes an infinite number of other events, all of which are set into motion by actors and objects that all have their own attributes.

You should be able to see very quickly how a simple event such as a specific book being borrowed occurs due to a complex chain of other events, and you can probably conceptualize that an infinite volume of data could never fully describe all those events and their attributes. It would be very easy to become overwhelmed, to become intellectually bogged in the complexity. Obviously, you need to avoid this.

The first step then to collecting the right data is to keep the business question in mind. There are many interesting detours and rabbit holes you can follow, but if they do not address a business question, then they are at best a distraction. You should be collecting data to either reveal an unknown that you need to know, or prove something that you need to prove. The big question then, is how much data

How Libraries Should Manage Data.
© 2016 Brian L. Cox. Published by Elsevier Ltd. All rights reserved.

do you need to achieve your goal, and from a cost perspective, what is the best compromise to ensure that the cost of collecting your data does not outweigh the benefits?

If you want to know how many people are using the collection, so as that you can show the accountants that you are busy, then you are not going to need very granular data. You will not care about who is borrowing (in relation to this question), you just want a total number for a quarter. In this instance, therefore, you will not need to know about most of the attributes associated with a borrowing event. If you have several libraries, you may wish to know how many items were borrowed at a specific location. Otherwise, it is most likely that you will only want to know how many books were borrowed per year.

In this example, there are only two attributes you need to worry about collecting data on in relation to a borrowing event, namely the year it happened in, and the location it occurred at. In almost all cases, I would expect that the library's management system software would produce aggregated reports that would answer this question, so you almost certainly will not have to worry about separately collecting this data. However, for arguments sake, let's say you did have to worry about this, and you are a small library, so you can use Excel to manage this.

So, theoretically assuming that you do have to manually record borrowing data, and you wanted to ensure you could easily run reports off your data, then how would you do this?

In this instance you would create a spreadsheet called "loans.xlsx," save it to the same folder where all your other statistics are to be kept, then rename "sheet 1" as "RawData." On the RawData tab you would type two headings, "Year," "Location," and "Number items borrowed." Under this you would enter the total items borrowed for each location for each year. It might look like this:

Year	Location	Number items borrowed
2015	Bigtownsville	576,975
2015	Suburbsville	71,117
2015	Tinysville	3,498

At any moment, if the Library Director wanted you do answer a question about how many items were borrowed in a year at a specific location, you could answer very quickly.

Now imagine the Library Director has come back to you and said, "I really need to know how many were borrowed in the last few years on a monthly basis. The Chief Administrator thinks even though our numbers are up for the year, that it was all due to the unusual influx of tourists in January. She claims she has been in the Library often, and is convinced that things are getting quieter. Now, this is obviously a silly scenario, but I am using it to convey an important point that might be lost in a more realistic, and therefore more complex scenario.

If the Library Director asked you this question, then you would not be able to answer it with the data at hand. If you could jump in a time machine and go back to when you first created the spreadsheet you could do one of two things. Firstly, you might create another spreadsheet, one for the month data, in addition to your spreadsheet for the year data. This is the stupid option. The other option is to redesign your raw data structure, so as that it can answer both questions from the one spreadsheet.

The purpose of this whole example is to get you to think about the how granular your data will need to be. If you aggregate up events, and enter them as a single number, then it becomes an omelet from which you will never be able to separate the yolk from the whites. Once you aggregated your borrowing events into a year, and entered that as a single number in your spreadsheet, then there is no way to dis-aggregate the data into months if the only data you have at your disposal is that spreadsheet into which you entered the yearly data. Consequently, when you are designing the structure of your RawData sheet, you need to think about the lowest possible level of data that your spreadsheet will need to report on, and ensure that level of data is captured. It is very easy to roll data up to a higher level — i.e., it is very easy to rollup monthly data into annual data. I will show you later how easy that is. However, it is impossible to drill down beyond your lowest level of data you have collected.

The "practical" lowest level of granularity you could possibly go to for a borrowing event is to have a row of data for each and every item borrowed. I put the work "practical" in quotation marks because it is not practical from a business perspective to manually collect this, but it is practical from a technical point of view. From a technical point of view, this would allow you to report on a whole host of things, such as the attributes of the borrower. How old was the person borrowing this book, have they borrowed in the past, if so how much. You could answer any question about the attributes of the borrower, if you collected that data. Of course, in practice, you could never enter this sort of information into a spreadsheet. However, this information is collected by your library management system, and depending upon its structure, it may or may not be accessible.

I have used the data automatically collected by the library management system at my institution to build a multidimensional data warehouse joining student usage of library resources, with student attributes such as their demographic profile and academic grades. To be clear, I did not actually create the cubes, this was done by the university's Performance Indicators Unit. But I did tell them what to do! The pertinent matter here is that if you did want to report on the relationship between grades and library use, then you will need very high resolution data.

How low do you go?

The degree of granularity you will need in your data depends on your business needs. This is of course the most unhelpful answer I could possibly provide. So I will help to point you in the right direction, but please remember, you will still need to think about what you need to measure in the context of your library's business needs. Also, personality invariably comes into play to some extent in every organization. What one Library Director considers important, another may not care about. The services provided by some libraries might be very different to others. And so on and so forth.

When it comes to collecting statistics, I gravitate toward the value proposition first, then consider the events associated with that value proposition, then consider the possible data needs in relation to that value proposition.

I am going to discuss borrowing, browsing, and visits, and for each discuss optimizing your data in the context of three important issues: variation; data structure; and avoiding false conclusions.

Measuring loans and accounting for variation

Unfortunately, in many cases there will be a limit on the amount of information you can extract from your library management system, so you might not be able to get all the information you need. Notwithstanding these limitations, you will probably need to answer a number of questions, such as:

- What areas of my collection are being heavily used — as I might want to extend this collection
- What areas of my collection are being under used — as I might want to try promoting these resources, or failing that weed them
- Did my promotion succeed in improving usage of library resources
- Is demand for my collection rising in general, or do I need to start to think about ways to add value

To answer these sort of questions you would need to collect data on:

- Date borrowed
- Location (if you have more than one library)
- Item's subject area

Even though it is unlikely that you could capture data at the transaction level, you should be able to still collect data that is granular enough to be able to determine whether a large scale promotion has been successful. You will need quite granular data for a few reasons. Firstly, you cannot expect a single promotion to result in widespread change in client behavior. Secondly, borrowing will vary over time even if you do nothing. You cannot assume that just because something went up, that it was because of your promotion, and similarly, just because it went down does not mean it failed.

At the very least, if you want assess the success of your promotions; you will need to collect daily statistics. To illustrate this, consider Promo Chart 1:

Promo Chart 1

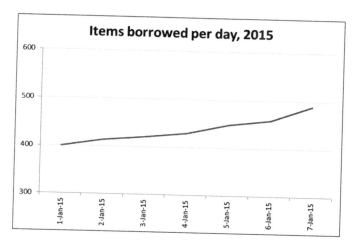

Imagine you ran a promotion on January 1, 2015. As you can see, the number of loans increased for several days after, almost by a whopping quarter by January 7, 2015. But what does that mean? It actually means nothing. You don't have enough data to be able to identify whether this movement is part of the normal variation in loans, or whether it is unusual. Things invariably change, regardless of whether you do something or not. If you do not promote the Library, loans may go up anyway. Similarly, they may also go down. You need to know whether the thing you did to promote the library was successful, but before you can do this you need to assess the change in your loans after the promotion, in the context of the normal variation in loans. For example, imagine you collected data for a further 3 months, and plotted that onto a chart.

Promo Chart 2

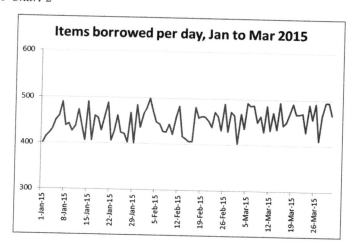

Unlike Promo Chart 1, which only showed 7 days' worth of data, the above chart shows 3 months' worth of data. The above chart also shows the number of loans is very volatile. This means the numbers change a lot from one day to the next. However, there is still a clearly visible pattern in this data. It would be impossible to predict what the exact number of loans would be for the next day in the series. However, in this dataset, there have never been less than 400 loans per day, or more than 500 loans per day. There are also enough data points to show that this is likely to be a reliable floor and ceiling for the data, and therefore, for the short term at least, it appears that there is sufficient trend in place to be able to predict with a reasonable degree of confidence that the loans are likely to reside somewhere between 400 and 500 items for the next day in the data series.

Consequently, taken in the context of the natural variation in loans, the upward trend shown in Promo Chart 1 was not something unusual or special. There are many other periods where loans increased for several days in a row. Moreover, these increases occurred well after the promotion was run on January 1, 2015, after many instances when loans had declined for several consecutive days. The above chart shows that the increase that did occur in the days following the promotion was within the normal background variation of loans per day. Therefore, there is no evidence that the promotion was successful, as loans may have increased anyway in the absence of the promotion.

There is no way of knowing for certain whether a change in the number of loans was something that would have occurred anyway, without any promotional activities, or whether the promotion did have an impact. There is ultimately no way of scientifically proving causality. However, you can prove that something did not work. If you had no loans before, and no loans after a promotion, then it's pretty safe to say it did not work. It is useful to know when something did not work, however, it's not a very motivating use of statistics.

Although it is not possible to prove scientifically with the data at hand whether a promotion caused increased usage, it is possible to identify from a practical point of view that the promotion most likely worked. The key is to identify the natural level of variation in loans, and looks for changes outside that variation.

Promo Chart 3

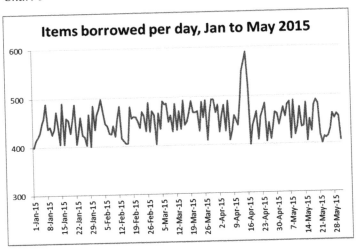

For example, in the above chart, loans were continuing to fluctuate between 400 and 500 items per day over the previous 4 months. Then on 13 April, you ran a promotion. On the day of the promotion loans broke through the 500 loan ceiling, and stayed above that ceiling for a few days before returning to the normal variation. If the promotion had not been run would this chart still contain the same spike? Maybe, maybe not. While existence of the spike is not enough evidence to write a scientific paper, it is enough to make a business decision.

Leadership is about making decisions based on imperfect information. If you waited for 100% certainty, you would rarely make a decision. And if 100% certainty was always obtainable within a reasonable amount of time, there would be no need for leadership; you would just chuck all the data into a machine, and the correct path to take would be spat out the other end. From a business perspective, the above chart is sufficient evidence that your promotion was most likely successful.

If you only collected your data at the month level, then you would not have seen that spike. For example, the data I used to generate the above chart is exactly the same as the data I used to generate Promo Chart 4.

Promo Chart 4

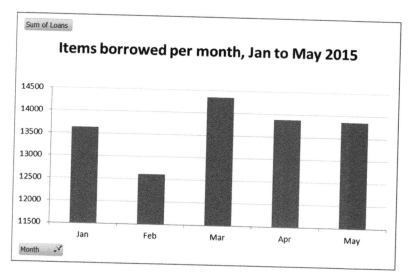

How could it be that on the daily level there was an increase in loans, but at the monthly level there was no increase? The answer is that the relatively small and short lived increase was swallowed up by the random background variation in loans. The point I am trying to make here is that in order to be able to determine if an individual promotion was successful, you will need to have quite granular data, most likely daily level data. Otherwise, you are going to have to employ a marketing genius, one that can achieve broad scale changes in client behavior across your whole client base. Good luck finding a marketing genius that you can afford!

In the real world, the best you are likely to achieve with your promotions is small scale temporary changes in behavior. If you know what specific promotion did and did not work, then you can fine tune your efforts, and hopefully, over time, the smaller efforts will work collectively to produce a much larger change.

There is another relevant point raised by the data. Notice how the number of loans varies in the above chart from one month to the next. Once again, this chart is based on the same numbers used to create Promo Chart 3. I produced this data by using the random Excel function to generate a random number between 400 and 500. I then manually entered the numbers for the week following the promotion, to generate the spike shown in Promo Chart 3. Consequently, aside from the five numbers for the promotion, the remaining 146 numbers for the days between 1 January and 31 May are random numbers between 400 and 500. This randomness is apparent in Promo Chart 3, but it is not apparent in the above chart. It would be very easy to try to read a trend in the above chart, particularly if you made a big effort in February to try to improve loans. People often unconsciously pick the facts that support their predetermined views. However, this is not a luxury you can afford, and is something you have to actively and consciously take steps to avoid.

The movement you see from one month to the next in Promo Chart 4 is a function of two things, the difference in total number of days in the month, and pure chance. Firstly, there are different number of days in each month. March, for example, has three more days than February, so naturally, it will tend to have a larger number. So, how much of the monthly variation in loans is due to there being a different number of days per month. Not much. You can hold the difference in the number of days in the month constant, by calculating the average number of items borrowed per day for a month.

Promo Chart 5

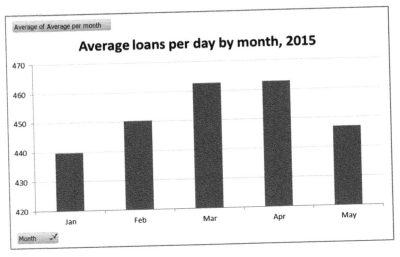

I used exactly the same data to create all the promo charts. This chart shows that even when the difference in the number of days a month is held constant, there are still differences from one month to the next. Indeed, it looks very much like a trend, but it is not. It is just some months have randomly had more items borrowed than other months. It is like throwing a whole heap of coins in the air, and seeing that a couple of them land near each other as heads. It is just chance, there is no greater meaning behind the results. In this instance I know it's chance, because I wrote the very simple Excel random formula. I did not know how the data would turn out, and the fact that this follows a nice curve is just luck, lucky in that it proves that randomness can generate patterns — which is the point I am trying to make.

So what do you do with this? Firstly, it shows that you need to ensure you at least look at the finest level of granular data before making decisions based on highly aggregated data. When you collect quite granular data (e.g., daily data), you will be able to see more easily the natural level of variation in whatever you are measuring. Since all the Promo Charts are created from the same raw dataset, you can deduce that the fluctuations in the monthly data are not significant. This also tells you that you need to collect data over a longer period, if you want to see the trends by month. I was curious to see just how many months' worth of random data I would need to produce before I could see the patterns that were obviously present in Promo Chart 3 also appear in data aggregated by month. It turns out you need a lot of data. Even with 2 years' worth of data, it is still not clearly obvious in the below chart that the loans data is simply based on a random value between 400 and 500. Now, imagine you are basing decisions on any of the charts other than Promo Chart 3, what is going to be the likely outcome?

Promo Chart 6

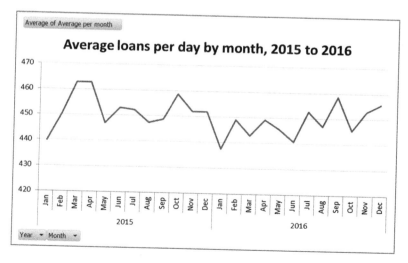

When the data is presented in this manner, the impact of the April 13, 2015 promotion is not visible either. However, there is much more to variability than just the mechanical fluctuations of numbers.

The world is full of fantastic books, and most of the good ones are in libraries. A good book that you should read is Edward Deming's book "Out of the Crisis." Yes, it was written in the 1980s, but it is still relevant. There are a lot of bread and butter basics that are still being ignored on a wide scale, and not just in the library sector. It is an easy read, and it is written by an internationally acclaimed author that is widely recognized as the father of modern quality management.

One of the key issues Deming discusses is variability in systems, and that if business decisions are to be driven by an informed understanding of your business, then understanding variability is essential. Unfortunately, I have not witnessed much focus on variability. Typically, many libraries tend to treat statistics as marketing fodder. Data is like a grab bag of goodies, from which the most positive stories are selected, and the less flattering statistics are pushed aside.

Of course, in the real world, marketing to stakeholders and clients is essential. If you don't do this you will sink. When I say that the energy of many libraries is focused primarily on looking good, that is not a euphemism for saying many Library Directors are narcissistic! There are many potential motives you might have for focusing on looking good, none of which need to have anything to do with narcissism:

- You may have lost the "strategic initiative." In other words, you may be so overwhelmed with the short term tactical issues, that you simply do not have the resources to dedicate to longer term real improvements. Obviously, if you are in this situation, you are in a downward spiral, and you need to find a way out no matter what it takes.
- You might be working in an organization or parent organization that has focused on looking good for decades. This long history might create the illusion that this sort of focus is productive and good management.
- You might believe so deeply in the value proposition of your library that you have an uncritical approach to your operations, and therefore your first instinct is to focus is on selling what you perceive as the clear and obvious benefits your organization provides to its clients.
- You might value strategy over operations. You might believe that process improvement is inward looking, and that the library needs to look outwards, to the new emerging technologies and opportunities. The first instinct of people with such a mindset will be to use operational data to showcase what the library has achieved, with the view to securing the political and resource capital for further expansion into new areas.

On this last point, a lot of staff that I have encountered tend to fall into one of three camps:

- The strategists. They give lip service to continuous improvement, but when they are being honest with themselves they consider it as inward looking, and antagonistic to innovation. They tend to always be looking around for the new technologies and options.
- The improvers. They tend to be inwardly focused, and look at refining their own processes, without lifting their head up for the broader view. When radical change does arrive, this group finds their whole world has been turned upside down.
- The "just get on with the job" crew. They are happy to continue with things exactly as they are, and sometimes can take an almost an anti-intellectual approach to strategy, and can be dismissive of process improvement. This can take many forms, and in libraries I have found it commonly expressed as a cottage industry type approach to work. They

cannot conceive as their work as a process (even though they will admit that most their day is spent doing things they have done before), and place enormous value on individual skills and knowledge. Therefore these people tend to see both strategy and process improvement as irrelevant. Their closest historical cousins are the artisans prior to the industrial revolution.

Now all the people who populate these groups are wonderful people, but together they create a system that is inherently conservative. The division of work into these compartments of thinking creates a system that stifles creativity. Where innovation does occur, it is usually because individuals have taken heroic steps to overcome great barriers. The success has been despite the system, not because of it.

To make progress, staff need to be all three of these people. They need to understand that the environment in which they work is dynamic and changing, and that these changes need to be anticipated, and new and shifting paths will need to be created to navigate the best way through these changes. Staff also need to understand that this does not diminish the importance of what we are doing right now. The ultimate driver of cost is what we do in the here and now, and therefore to free up resources to do be able to do the new things that will need to be done, we need to look at the processes we doing right now. The cost of being inefficient now is a reduction in future choices. Lastly, staff need to be content in what they are doing — this does not mean enjoying doing the same thing for years, very few people enjoy that. It means finding value in the present, and using that to gain satisfaction, and invigorate ourselves.

If a library was populated with staff members who are able to have each of these three personalities living in each of them, then the possibilities will be great. However, if the library is populated by people that only possess one of these personalities, then the sum will be less than its parts. The strategic thinkers will ignore process, the process improvers will be disconnected with the strategists, and the bulk of people just trying to do their day-to-day work will see both camps as being irrelevant.

What has this got to do with variability? Firstly, variability can exist in many forms, and not just in things that are easy to count. People vary too, both between and within individuals. If you do not have systems in place to control variability, then it is likely that the variability in staff aptitude, expertise and knowledge, will also be reflected in the variability of the turnaround time, quality, and quantity of the services provided.

Deming argued that the key to improving many systems is to understand the nature of this variability, study potential root causes from a holistic perspective, and involve all staff in making experimental changes to workflow, procedures, training and so forth, in a collective attempt to improve quality and efficiency by reducing variability. Right now you might be thinking, who cares about variability with things like turnaround time if your overall average is fine, and has been improving. I would respond, sure, if you are 90% concerned about looking good, then there is no need to dig deeper. However, if you are 90% concerned about being good, and you know that if you look after the company the stock price will follow with minimal marketing effort, then the average figures are not good enough.

If you have a high level of variability in your system, this means you do not have the system under control, and therefore the results you are getting from the system have nothing to do with your management style, and everything to do with individual differences between your staff. For example, say you do a lot of original cataloging, and you are finding that there is a wide variation in turnaround time from one staff member to the next. Let's also say that you accounted for the variation in complexity of jobs, and still found this high level of variation. What this probably means is that some staff are highly efficient, and others are not so efficient. This is to be expected, only one person can come first in a race, and you will always have staff ability distributed across a bell curve of productivity. It is also possible that the variation in turnaround time is a by-product of variation in the quality of outputs. In this case, the variation still exists, it just exists in a different form, i.e., quality instead of quantity. Now, under such a system, if it is performing well the manager might try to take credit. But what are they taking credit for? They have high levels of variation, which logically means that the performance difference is due to differences in staff ability, which in turn comes down to the natural variation in people. Under this situation, if you are performing well it is largely a product of luck, you have just been lucky enough to hire a few more people with aptitudes on the right side of the bell curve. At best you can thank your HR people, but if overall the aptitudes of people that they have recruited reflect the general population, then not even HR can take credit. It has just been luck, and you have been lucky. If you want to improve a system, the first step is to get it under control, which means reducing variation. Once you have reduced variation, then you can look at the next cycle of improvement.

Consequently, if you are in the camp of people that are 90% concerned about being good, and only 10% focused on looking good, then data is going to play a starring role in your library. Data will be center field, and you will collect data on all your processes, and use that data to understand variability, get your processes under control, and use the data to inform continuous improvement. Starting this journey requires highly focused and disciplined leadership. Sustaining this journey requires the leadership to grow their staff to the point where they can take ownership and control over continuous improvement.

On this last point, continuous improvement and strategy often compete in an antagonistic relationship. The truth is, however, it is not only possible, but necessary, to do both things simultaneously. To repeat myself, the cost of being inefficient now is a reduction in future choices. Inefficiency restricts strategic choice like cholesterol; thickening, hardening, and ultimately narrowing arteries.

Visits and how to organize the data into columns

It is no good having great granular data that you could use to answer pressing business questions, if you do not structure your data correctly. If the data is well structured, then it will be possible to slice and dice your data like a master chef.

Good data structure starts with columns. Do *not* enter your data into cross tabs, such as the below.

Month	Location			
	Bigtownsville	Suburbsville	Tinysville	Total
Jan	13,907	7,589	202	21,698
Feb	86,990	2,126	391	89,507
Mar	58,438	6,810	45	65,293
Apr	4,528	7,319	346	12,193
May	43,113	6,114	386	49,613
Jun	76,814	9,905	405	87,124
Jul	40,563	5,102	421	46,086
Aug	64,051	6,631	398	71,080
Sep	64,259	3,109	108	67,476
Oct	1,308	7,419	118	8,845
Nov	82,322	1,259	476	84,057
Dec	40,682	7,734	202	48,618
Total	576,975	71,117	3,498	651,590

As discussed in the beginning of this chapter, this structure makes it impossible to report on anything but the most simple of things.

To structure your data properly you will need a column for each variable, and the header for that column will describe those variables. I could talk about not using variables as dimensions, but I don't need to, as there is a much simpler solution. Always aim to have your raw data occupying as few columns as possible. Take the visit statistics. You could create a column for each location, as per the below table, which would in effect result in something looking very much like the above table.

Year	Month	Bigtownsville	Suburbsville	Tinysville
2015	Jan	13907	7589	202
2015	Feb	86990	2126	391
2015	Mar	58438	6810	45

This might be the most intuitive option, and one that many people gravitate toward. However, this will have four drawbacks. Say you open a new library, or close an existing location. What do you do with the data? If you added a location you would have to add a new column, which means you might have to rebuild your formulas, and the pivots. Secondly, you will need to create a column to sum all the locations, if you want to be able to easily create pivots that show the total number of visits across all locations. This might seem easy enough, but if you add a total column, then later when you build a pivot table you would also be creating measures that do not have scope over any of the locations, and the locations could not be used as filters for this measure (this will make sense after reading the Pivot chapter). Finally, you will end up with a messy and confusing spreadsheet, with way too many columns, with some of the column headings actually being variables, which will only confuse the users of the pivot tables. Moreover, these dimensions may be subject to change, only further compounding the confusion.

Adding each location as a new column is about as elegant as a hippo in a tutu. The best solution for capturing information on the various library site locations is to add a column, called for example, "Location," and users enter the site location in that column. Using this approach you can add a new location without affecting the data structure at all.

Date	Location	Number
1-Jan-15	Bigtownsville	442
1-Jan-15	Suburbsville	492
1-Jan-15	Tinysville	77
2-Jan-15	Bigtownsville	454
2-Jan-15	Suburbsville	275
2-Jan-15	Tinysville	184

In this example, the data has been taken to the day level of granularity. The day level of information will help you with identifying the success of promotions, rostering, and communication opportunities. Chances are the Director is only interested in the higher level data. However, it is very easy to roll this data up to the month, quarter, year, or whatever period you wish.

If the data has to be entered manually, there is a good chance that some of the staff responsible for data entry will make it clear that they are unhappy with the changes. The bottom line is it will require them to enter more data. For example, if Bigtownsville was in a column all by itself, then the staff entering data for Bigtownsville would only have to enter the number of visits. Under the revised structure they will have to enter the date and the location as well as the number of visits. Depending upon the outlook of the staff member, they might see this as managerial stupidity, and a waste of their time. However, if we cannot get data out, then it is a complete waste of their time no matter how efficiently they enter the data. Of course you can always get some data out, but the barriers and time involved in doing so will ensure that only the simplest of data is reported on, and being so simple it will not tell you anything you don't already know. Your first job is to make the data usable, and only after you have done that can you focus on making data entry easy. It is a complete false economy to do things the other way around.

Most libraries should have a gate sensor that feeds information into a database. If this is the case, then you should be able to extract very granular data, right down to the hour of the visit, automatically, with very little manual data manipulation. Chances are it will not take much extra effort to export the most granular level of data available, in which case you should do so.

There is always a legitimate use for knowing what hours of the day the library is busier. For example, say you are considering changing opening hours or you wish to run an event and want to ensure that it is well attended; in both cases knowing the actual patterns of visits will help you to make more informed decisions.

Browsed items and avoiding false conclusions

If you can retrieve the bibliographic details of an item using a scanner, then it is possible that with little effort you could collect very granular data on browsed items. Remember, however, you do not want to add to the fog of irrelevant data. Just because you can collect that data, does not mean that you should. Unless it adequately addresses one of your data selection criteria, then it is wasteful to collect this data.

It is possible to conceive of some situations where a high level of granularity of browsing data might be useful. If your library is very much focused on delivering value through your monograph collection, and a lot of the material is very expensive reference material that is not available for loan, then you would probably want to know whether that collection is in demand. Scanners here could be used during the re-shelving process to collect data. In this case, you would need a spreadsheet that would contain a row for every instance where a book was re-shelved. The type of additional information you can collect will depend upon the attributes you can associate with the call number, and might potentially include the subject matter, the location of the item, and the cost of the item. The scanner should be driven off software that can automatically write other data to your table, such as the time/date the material was scanned. Scanners are inexpensive now, and the software to drive them is not that complex, so if this is something that would help you to answer critical business questions, then it would be worth at least exploring.

The information you collect from scanning browsed items could help you with things such as:

- identifying how much it costs to make these works accessible (i.e., this is one facet of effort)
- identifying trends in busy times, which may help with rostering (another facet of effort)
- identifying when there are higher levels of demand, which will be useful for marketing (see previous discussion on loans)

By themselves, the browsed statistics collected from the scanner can *never* tell you:

- the clients' perceived value of that book
- whether the client objectively benefited from reading that book (obviously, this is an irrelevant question for fictional works)

These last points are important. I have found many people have difficulty differentiating between demand for a service and the value being delivered by that service. I think this probably stems from a deeply held belief that the library services are intrinsically valuable, therefore if someone uses it, it automatically follows that they are benefiting from using it. This is a fallacy. You can decide to ignore this fallacy when it comes to things like showcasing your library to stakeholders and administrators, and that is perfectly understandable in the context of limited information about value and outcomes. However, if you want to use demand type statistics convincingly, and you want to use them to inform strategic decisions and drive improvements, then you need to be conscious of their limitations, and understand the difference between demand and value.

Most people, including myself, can find it difficult to shift their thinking on matters that are based upon deeply held assumptions. The belief that demand and value are inseparable is one of those assumptions that I have encountered with many librarians over many years. It takes many forms, from the more obvious "they are attending our information literacy classes therefore they are benefiting" to the much more subtle "demand for library space is a reasonable proxy measure for the value of the space". The best way to rattle these assumptions loose, so as that they can be examined critically, is to use analogies where the underlying logic is similar, but because the subject matter has been changed any emotional investment is removed. So, if you don't like analogies, bad luck!

Let's say there is a bookshop that is getting a lot of visitors, and for the sake of clarity let's say this is happening in the 1980s, before visiting stores became a common foreplay prior to making online purchases. Let's also say this bookstore never sells a single book. Their business model will float or swim based on their profitability, so it does not matter how many visits they get, if they do not sell books eventually they will end up having to permanently close shop. Now, you might think what sort of a bookshop could possibly be in that situation. If you think this, the likely culprit is that you consider books to have such intrinsic value, that you cannot possibly imagine a bookstore full of visitors but not making any sales. So, if this describes you, try imagining a different store, say one that sells brick-a-brack. I have seen plenty of these types of shops, having been dragged into them by my partner from time to time. She never purchases anything, does a quick loop and she's out (thank god!). In all my years I have never seen anyone buy anything at these shops, and I have often seen them fold. Why? Because the people entering these stores don't find anything of value. They might pick stuff up, turn it around in their hands, look at it closely, and then put it back on the shelf. The only value the shop provided was to satisfy a temporary curiosity for window shoppers; window shoppers who were only willing to pay for that value with a small amount of their time. Visits does not automatically equate to meaningful value.

As I discussed in the first chapter, this is not a book about what to measure, it's a book about how to do it efficiently and effectively. But if you are going to measure efficiently and effectively, you cannot think you are measuring value when you are not. Why should you care about this? Your current performance measures may be marching in locked step with the value you perceive you are offering now, however, what happens if the two diverge at some point in the future?

Imagine a simple world were people believed that wearing larger shoes improved your IQ. This is a silly world to be sure, but sometimes a silly analogy is required to dislodge a deeply held belief. Imagine Jane owns a shoe shop, and Jane has based all her business decisions, including marketing, inventory, and training on the deeply and uncritically held belief that by selling a client larger shoes, she was helping to improve their IQ. One day, a competitor, Sally, realizes no one likes floppy ill-fitting shoes, and develops a line of comfortable shoes that fit properly. Before Sally attempts to sell the shoes, she starts a big marketing campaign, in which she demonstrates that the increase in IQ is not caused by wearing larger shoes, but by growing older. Imagine this marketing was very effective, and people suddenly realized that larger shoes did not help them to become smarter. The previous fashions that included huge shoes are now widely perceived to be ridiculous, and the rapidly diminishing number of people that continue to wear oversized shoes are subject to reactions ranging from pity to snide derision. The value Jane thought she was providing was not the value she actually did provide. She was not improving IQ, the value she was providing was enabling a misconception. Jane has two options, she can hang onto her old belief that big shoes contribute to improved IQ, or she can adjust her value proposition and performance measures accordingly.

The moral to the story is that if you are uncritical of your value proposition and you consume the performance indicators that fit the story of how you would like things to be, then you cannot complain if business circumstances change radically, and you are left behind. It would obviously be very silly for Jane to fail to recognize the changes around her, and grab onto any short term improvement in statistics as evidence that the change is a short lived fad. It would also be equally silly for Jane to put a positive spin on every bit of negative data, no amount of spin will save her situation in the long run. However, it is easy to be critical of Jane; we are emotionally removed from the situation. It is not so easy when you are living in the change, and are emotionally invested in the situation. Jane can only survive if she can look at the situation objectively, and not let her emotional investment in the history of her store slow her down. The same is true for everyone else, including librarians. To survive rapid change, Jane needs to understand the value proposition of her store in the context of social change, and base that understanding on objective data. The problem for libraries when it comes to measuring value is the lack of a price signal. When someone buys something, they are ascribing value; whether it is a conscious decision, or not, and whether it is rational, or not. Almost everyone on the planet has a very small pool of money, and so when they spend some of it, they are making choices. If they choose to buy one thing, then that's less money available to spend on other things. From an economic perspective, this is called an opportunity cost. The amount of money individuals are willing to part with to get something gives a rough indication of the value of that thing to that person. I say rough, because most people are not "rational economic actors." You might buy something on impulse and regret it later; because you failed to contemplate the full range of other commodities or services you could have procured for the same amount, and perhaps delivered more value for you. How is this relevant to libraries? Well, if the almost the entire planet's resource allocation is being determined on the basis of the collective price signals sent by individual's purchasing patterns; then libraries are operating in an orbit outside of that model. Aside from a membership fee, most libraries provide free access. This means users don't have to make choices about their money, only their time. Consequently, when libraries talk about value they are talking in a different language to that being used globally to make decisions about resource allocation. You need to be conscious of this if you are to use your data effectively.

To illustrate just how different this language is, please indulge me with one more silly analogy, and imagine you have been teleported to an island where 99 people only speak mathematics, and you are the only person that speaks emotion. If you want to communicate with the mathematicians, then you will need to find a common language. But what are the chances that they will make the effort to learn emotion, after all there are 99 of them, and only one of you. Why should 99 people change to make one person happy? They are quite content speaking mathematics, it has served them well. Moreover, even if they could learn emotion, it is such a leap from what they are currently speaking, such a vast gulf between you, that they are unlikely to be able to speak it properly anyway. Meaning, for example, is a meaningless concept to the mathematicians; you might as well be trying to teach a person who has been blind from birth the meaning of color. The same applies to you. You might try to learn to speak mathematics, but if you have only ever spoken emotion, then it will be incredibly difficult, and there is such a big risk that if you get it wrong the mathematicians will not understand the difficulties and challenges you face in communicating, and simply write you off as being simple. The biggest risk though, is if you don't understand how truly different the languages you speak are, and proceed as if there is no difference.

How you decide to measure value is up to you, but do not think for a moment that ascribing economic value is a matter of simply "translating" existing statistics into classic business terms, or that it is possible to artificially inject a price signal into your data. For example, if people had to pay for a library, then despite all the contingent valuations that have been in vogue, I honestly doubt many people would pay in practice. If people were willing to pay the full cost for using their libraries, then there would be a chain McLibraries around the world. If money can be made out of something, then that niche will be quickly filled. But there are no McLibraries. This is not surprising, when much of the value of the library is wrapped up it being free. Of course, someone has to pay, and in this instance it's the taxpayer. From an economic rationalist's point of view, that might be evidence that the library sector was not delivering value; if it could not succeed in getting its users to pay the costs of its services, then it cannot be delivering value to those users. And this is the key point. The language differences between public goods and the free market are so great that if you are to succeed in convincing decision makers on the value of libraries, it will be because you have succeed in shifting the way value is conceived by those decision makers, at least with respect to libraries. You cannot succeed at this by being oblivious to what your measures are actually counting, or by deluding yourself into believing that it is simply a matter of tweaking a few words, and the method of measurement.

When I visited Oxford University Library, to me the overwhelming sense of history instantly made any economic rationalist argument about the value of the space patently crude and irrelevant. Understanding such value required more than words on a page. I needed to experience Oxford University Library to understand its value. I needed to see it, to be there. Not everyone can be Oxford, so dragging decision makers into your library might not help you. However, you may well provide value that cannot be described in standard economic language. If you are in this situation, then how would you communicate that value to decision makers? This is the hard question you have to answer, and you will never be able to find that answer by blindly fumbling, grabbing at any and all data that comes within arm's reach. Know your value proposition first, have a strategy to communicate that value proposition; then, and only then, focus on collecting the right data.

Getting the most out of your raw data

5

Some readers might think there is a tension between capturing data to drive contin-uous improvement, and lifting the fog of irrelevant data. They might think, hang on a second, didn't you spend a whole chapter talking about putting your data on a diet? Then in the previous chapter you spoke about needing to understand variabil-ity, which requires more sophisticated data collection. Yes, I did say both things, but no, there is no contradiction. If you take a shotgun approach to collecting data to inform continuous improvement, then yes, you will be hitting a whole heap of irrelevant targets, and in the process just adding confusion. The data you collect for informing continuous improvement needs to be deliberate; it needs to be targeted. To continue with the analogy of data fitness, once you have got rid of all the fat, the next step is to build muscle. Unfortunately, this is where the analogy breaks down, because where you can build muscle and lose fat simultaneously, for data you need to take a much more linear approach. If you don't get rid of the irrelevant stuff first, then you will not be able to spot the useful stuff. If you present staff with half a dozen performance measures, all telling a slightly different story, then it will probably lead to confusion, or at the very least create a wide variation in under-standing of what the measures actually mean for the team and the process. The beauty of creating a robust raw data structure is that you can easily report on the one or two indicators for a process, while at the same time having access to a greater depth of information to identify variation and system performance. Consequently, both the structure and content of your raw data is king, and how you report on that data will determine whether it helps to achieve positive change, or just add to a fog of confusion.

Once you have organized the data into a usable structure, the next step is to use Excel's power to build on the data so that you can identify things such as system variability. Excel has incredible power, and even if you only use a fraction of this power you will be able to maximize the amount of useful information you can get out of a given dataset.

To get the most out of your raw data you will have to do a few things:

- You will have to know how to write good formulas, which means short and simple formulas
- You will need to know how to copy these formulas quickly to other cells and ranges
- You will have to learn, practice, and understand ten key formulas
- You will have to understand the error messages your formulas might generate from time-to-time

This chapter will discuss how to do the above.

Keep it simple stupid!

Excel formulas can scare many people. If you are one of those people, the thing to remember is your fear is based on an illusion. **ALL** formulas are very simple when broken down into their component parts. For example, say you have raw data for visits that looks something like the below. This is of course only a snippet, so pretend that you have years' worth of data.

Date	Location	Number
1-Jan-15	Bigtownsville	442
1-Jan-15	Suburbsville	492
1-Jan-15	Tinysville	77
2-Jan-15	Bigtownsville	454
2-Jan-15	Suburbsville	275
2-Jan-15	Tinysville	184

Chances are you would like to aggregate the data by Month and Year. The simplest way to do this is to add a column called "Year," and another called "Month." You should never ask the user to enter something that can be generated by a formula, and given you can calculate the month and the year from the date, you must use formulas. The formulas for Year and Month are very simple:

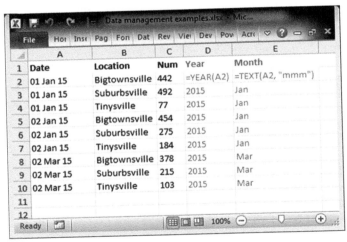

Month looks a bit different to Year for a reason. If you typed the formula = MONTH(A2) in the first row, you would get the number 1. If the date had been 7 Mar 15, then the formula would return the number 3. The MONTH() formula returns a number between 1 and 12, which represents the month of the year.

When it comes to pivot tables, for the most part you get out what you put in. So if you have months listed as numbers between 1 and 12, then when you aggregate the data by month, that is what you will see — i.e., numbers between 1 and 12.

Some people may be fine with this, but a lot of people, including myself, would probably not like it. I prefer to see the months in their text form, preferably abbreviated to three letters, e.g., "Jan", "Feb", "Mar," etc. It makes tables easier to read, and makes it instantly clear that the data refers to month, and not something else.

So, if you wanted to have the months displayed in text form, then there are many ways to do this. There will be the simplest way to write the formula, and an infinite number of more complex forms of the formula. The simplest way, I think, is the formula I have used above. What the TEXT formula does is take a value from a cell, and reformat it according to your specifications.

Paradoxically, it is actually pretty easy to write unnecessarily complex formulas, and here are two examples that will do the same as =TEXT(A2, "mmm"):

- = IF(A2 = 1, "Jan", IF(A2 = 2, "Feb", IF(A2 = 3, "Mar", IF(A2 = 4, "Apr", IF(A2 = 5, "May", IF(A2 = 6, "Jun", IF(A2 = 7, "Jul", IF(A2 = 8, "Aug", IF(A2 = 9, "Sep", IF (A2 = 10, "Oct", IF(A2 = 11, "Nov", "Dec")))))))))))
- = VLOOKUP(A2, $V$2:$W$13, 2, FALSE)

The measure of your talent as a formula writer is not whether you have produced something so complicated that it makes people stand back with fear, spontaneously put their hands over their mouths while whispering "oh my god!" You have failed if the next person taking over your role is reduced to adopting the fetal position upon realizing what they have inherited. A good formula is short, it is elegant, it does what it needs to do with the maximum clarity possible. Clearly, the above two formulas fail! They will return the correct results, but will require a lot more computing power to do it, and they will be difficult to change later given their purpose is so opaque. The first formula uses nested if statements to test if a certain number is present, then it return a corresponding month text value if true, otherwise if false it cascades down to the next if statement. There are so many nested if statements that this formula may not even work on earlier versions of Excel.

The second formula is shorter, but is still more complicated than it needs to be. Firstly, it requires you to create another table that defines the text value for each number value for a given month:

Month (number)	Month (text)
1	Jan
2	Feb
3	Mar
4	Apr
5	May
6	Jun
7	Jul
8	Aug
9	Sep
10	Oct
11	Nov
12	Dec

VLOOKUPs are very useful, and frequently unavoidable, and I will explain more about them shortly. However, avoid them if you can, as they can slow a spreadsheet down if it contains thousands of rows of data.

So, when you write a formula, unless you are very proficient with Excel, or it is blindingly obvious that the formula is as simple as it can be — you really should google what other functions are available that will do the trick. There are chat forums out there for every fetish, hobby, interest, and job imaginable. Whatever your question is, thousands of people have had the same question before, and at least half a dozen of them have submitted the question to an online forum. It will not take much effort to find useful information, you just have to look. Lucky you are a librarian, so you know how and where to look!

Make it easy stupid! Absolute and relative formulas

This is about making things easy on you. There are a number of ways to make your job a whole lot easier. The best and most frequent time saver you will ever use is the $ symbol in your formulas. When you write a formula, you can of course copy it to other cells, rather than retyping it every time. You can copy it to other cells by using the copy and paste method, or you can do it using the fill method. The fill method is the fastest way of copying formulas. To use this function, you simply select the cell that contains the formula you want to copy, and all the cells you want to copy the formulas to, then select either fill down, fill up, fill left, or fill right — depending on which direction you want to copy the formulas. For the sake of using an example, let's say we have a library that for some reason has library buildings scattered in some of the world's biggest cities. And for some reason you have ignored everything I have said about structuring raw data, and have decided to enter your data directly into a crosstab. In this instance you are counting the number of items loaned per quarter. And, yes, they are small numbers, but that is karma for bad data structure! Say you wanted to know the total for each location. That's easy enough, just sum cells B2 to E2.

	A	B	C	D	E	F
1		Jan - Mar	Apr - Jun	Jul - Sep	Oct - Dec	Total
2	Washington	217	205	207	207	=SUM(B2:E2)
3	London	101	119	137	109	
4	New York	48	78	94	56	
5	Paris	91	88	90	86	
6	Berlin	95	118	104	119	
7						

If you wanted to copy that formula down, for all the other locations, the easiest way to do this is to select cells F2 to F6, and select "Fill down" from the appropriate menu. I will not say where this menu is, because it changes with different versions of Excel. Alternatively, most versions of Excel have the same shortcut. If you press the Ctrl key, and the D key at the same time, it will fill down (Ctrl + D).

	A	B	C	D	E	F
1		Jan - Mar	Apr - Jun	Jul - Sep	Oct - Dec	Total
2	Washington	217	205	207	207	=SUM(B2:E2)
3	London	101	119	137	109	
4	New York	48	78	94	56	
5	Paris	91	88	90	86	
6	Berlin	95	118	104	119	
7						
8						

This is very simple, and most people will know how to do this. The next short cut is also very simple, but I have found a surprising number of staff that don't use it.

When you fill a formula down, Excel will change the ranges in your formula to match what it thinks you want.

	A	B	C	D	E	F
1		Jan - Mar	Apr - Jun	Jul - Sep	Oct - Dec	Total
2	Washington	217	205	207	207	=SUM(B2:E2)
3	London	101	119	137	109	=SUM(B3:E3)
4	New York	48	78	94	56	=SUM(B4:E4)
5	Paris	91	88	90	86	=SUM(B5:E5)
6	Berlin	95	118	104	119	=SUM(B6:E6)

For example, when I used fill down on the highlighted range, Excel adjusted the row reference. So in row 3, the formula sums the values in row 3, not row 2. This is exactly what we wanted. For example, we would not want cell F3 to sum the values in row 2. However, there are times when this behavior is not helpful.

Say we wanted to create a percentage column. You could do this by entering the below formula in cell G2 (note, by setting the number format to percentage you don't have to multiply the result by 100).

Now, if you select fill down (Ctrl + D), Excel will not do what you hoped for. See how the formula in G4 in the below image is dividing cell F4 by F9. Cell F4 is fine, but F9 is not. Excel has done this because when you fill down it simply increments the row and column references relative to the cell containing the formula.

	A	B	C	D	E	F	G
1		Jan - Mar	Apr - Jun	Jul - Sep	Oct - Dec	Total	Percentage
2	Washington	217	205	207	207	=SUM(B2:E2)	=F2/F7
3	London	101	119	137	109	=SUM(B3:E3)	=F3/F8
4	New York	48	78	94	56	=SUM(B4:E4)	=F4/F9
5	Paris	91	88	90	86	=SUM(B5:E5)	=F5/F10
6	Berlin	95	118	104	119	=SUM(B6:E6)	=F6/F11
7	Total	=SUM(B2:B6)	=SUM(C2:C6)	=SUM(D2:D6)	=SUM(E2:E6)	=SUM(F2:F6)	=SUM(G2:G6)
8							
9							
10							

There are a few ways to deal with this, including the good, the bad, and the ugly. The ugly way is to manually type in each formula. Don't do that. The bad way, at least in this instance, would be to use a named range for cell F7 (i.e., the total). The good way is to use the $ sign in your formula.

The $ sign says to Excel, this is an absolute address, please don't try to be clever when I fill my cells down (or up, etc.), just use the same reference point. In this example, we don't want Excel to be clever with row 7. The solution, then is to put a $ sign in front of the 7, so as that your first formula in cell G2 looks like this: =F2/F$7. Now, when you select the cells you want to copy this formula to, and select fill down, Excel does what you want it to. All the formulas, from G2 to G6 now divide the row total by the grand total (i.e., cell F7).

A	B	C	D	E	F	G
1	Jan - Mar	Apr - Jun	Jul - Sep	Oct - Dec	Total	Percentage
2 Washington	217	205	207	207	=SUM(B2:E2)	=F2/F$7
3 London	101	119	137	109	=SUM(B3:E3)	=F3/F$7
4 New York	48	78	94	56	=SUM(B4:E4)	=F4/F$7
5 Paris	91	88	90	86	=SUM(B5:E5)	=F5/F$7
6 Berlin	95	118	104	119	=SUM(B6:E6)	=F6/F$7
7 Total	=SUM(B2:B6)	=SUM(C2:C6)	=SUM(D2:D6)	=SUM(E2:E6)	=SUM(F2:F6)	=SUM(G2:G6)

Once you get the hang of when to use absolute addresses in your formulas (i.e., the $ sign), and when to use relative addressing (i.e., no $ sign), you will find that you can fill a spreadsheet with formulas very quickly and efficiently. On that note, you can toggle between relative and absolute addressing in formulas by using the F4 key, but you have to be editing the formula for this to work.

Formulas you must know

There are a few formulas that you absolutely must know. If you can count, add, subtract, and divide, then you will be fine. And if you can read, then you will be able to understand the logical formulas, such as IF, AND, OR. Even the most complex formula imaginable is simply a collection of these simple building blocks. Get to know these building blocks, and you will be fine.

SUM. This is an Excel classic, the go to formula that you will no doubt be visiting frequently. You can sum individual cells, or ranges. For example:

	A	B	C
1	1	12	=SUM(A1:B1)
2	2	13	=SUM(A1:A5)
3	3	14	=SUM(A1,A3,A5)
4	4	15	=SUM(A1:B5)
5	5	16	=SUM(A1:B3,A5:B5)

Notice there are five different examples of sum ranges. The formula in C1 sums across the columns, the next formula sums across the rows, the third sums a series of individual cells, the forth sums the whole block of numbers (A1 to B5) and the fifth formula sums two different blocks of cells. In other words, the sum function is very flexible, and this same flexibility applies to many formulas. The things you are summing do not have to be all grouped together.

COUNT. This formula counts the number of values in a range. It comes in four flavors: a formula that will only count cells containing numbers, and a formula that will count cells that contain anything, a formula that counts blanks, and a formula that will only count things under certain circumstances.

	A	B	C	D
1	1	=COUNT(A1:A6)	= 3	I only count numbers
2	2	=COUNTA(A1:A6)	= 4	I count the number of non-empty cells
3	don't fall asleep reading this	=COUNTBLANK(A1:A6)	= 2	I count the number of empty cells
4	4			
5				
6				
7				

The above is reasonably self-explanatory, but if you are unsure, simply open up a spreadsheet, and type in the above. If you change the values in column A, e.g., delete the value in cell A1, you will see the formula returns a different result. Experimenting like this is a fantastic way to learn when you are unsure.

IF. This formula uses logic to test whether something is true or false, and then do one thing if it is true, and do a different thing if it is false. For example, if we wanted to have text to show whether Sally received more awards on average, then we might use the following formula:

	A	B
1	Number of times Sally Smith received "Librarian of the Year" award	3
2	Average number of times everyone else received "Librarian of the Year" award	1
3		
4		
5	=IF(B1>B2, "Sally is above average", "Sally is below average")	
6	= Sally is above average	
7		

The formula used in this example is: $= IF(B1 > B2,$ "Sally is above average," "Sally is below average"). The formula structure for IF is: IF(logical test, value if true, value if false).

So, in this example, the first part of the formula is the logical test is "$B1 > B2$." In effect, this formula is asking "is this equation correct?" In this example $B1 = 3$, and $B2 = 1$. Therefore when those values are plugged into the equation, the result is $3 > 1$. This statement is true, three is greater than one. Because the statement is true, the IF formula goes off and does the thing specified in the "value if true" section of the formula. In this example, the value if true is "Sally is above average." If B2 contained the value 4, then the statement "3 is greater than 4" would be false. In this case, because the statement is false, the IF formula will return whatever you plugged into the "value if false" section of the formula.

However, what if both B1 and B2 contained 3? The formula would return "Sally is below average," which is not correct. The formula would do this because the statement "3 is greater than 3" is incorrect, and therefore the formula would default to the "value if false" section of the formula. This means you need another IF statement in this formula, to deal with the possibility that B1 = B2. To do this, you will need to create what is called "nested" IF statements. The formula will look like this:

	A	B
1	Number of times Sally Smith received "Librarian of the Year" award	3
2	Average number of times everyone else received "Librarian of the Year" award	3
3		
4		
5	=IF(B1=B2,"Sally is average",IF(B1>B2,"Sally is above average","Sally is below average"))	
6	= Sally is average	

The first part of the formula tests whether B1 = B2. If this statement is true, then the formula will return "Sally is average." If it is not true, then the formula will go to the "value if false" section of the formula. This section happens to be another IF formula, and hence the term nested IF statements. The "value if false" section of this equation is simply the first IF equation we discussed.

AND and OR. As librarians you will be very familiar with Boolean operators. You can use these in Excel too. The structure of AND and OR are the same, so for brevity I will simply refer to AND. The AND formula returns true or false, and is structured like this: AND(logical test 1, logical test 2, etc.).

This is probably not very helpful, so here is an example. Imagine you are considering buying an ice cream, and your decision was based on three things, is it hot, do I have time to eat it, and do I have spare change. Your AND formula would look like this: AND(is it hot, do I have time to eat, do I have spare change). If all those conditions are met, then the formula will return true; if even one of them is false (e.g., its not a hot day), then the formula will return false. This formula is particularly useful when used in conjunction with the IF statement. For example IF(AND(is it hot, do I have time to eat, do I have spare change), buy an ice cream [value if true section of IF formula], do not buy an ice cream [value if false section of IF formula]). Of course this is a silly formula that you could not actually plug into Excel, but the structure is the same. Here is a real example.

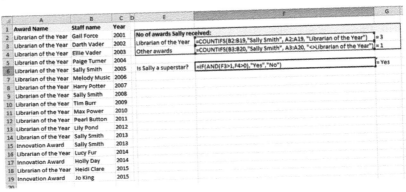

The formula is: = IF (AND(F3 > 1, F4 > 0),"Yes", "No"). The first part of the formula is the logical test, which in this case is an AND statement. If the AND statement returns true, then the IF formula will go to the "value if true" section of the formula, which happens to contain the value "Yes." If the AND statement returns false, then the IF formula will go to the section dealing with "value if false," which in this example contains the value "No." In this example the AND statement is essentially asking, did Sally get more than one librarian of the Year award, and at least one other award. If this is true, then she is a superstar, if not, then she is not a superstar.

COUNTIF. This formula is a little bit more complicated than COUNT, but not by much. COUNTIF comes in two flavors: the simple version; and the extended version.

	A	B	C	D	E	F	G	
1	Award Name	Staff name	Year					
2	Librarian of the Year	Gail Force	2001				=COUNTIF(B2:B19, "Sally Smith")	=4
3	Librarian of the Year	Darth Vader	2002		Sally Smith		=COUNTIF(B2:B19,E3)	=4
4	Librarian of the Year	Ellie Vader	2003		Sally Smith	Librarian of the Year	=COUNTIFS(B2:B19, E4, A2:A19, F4)	=3
5	Librarian of the Year	Paige Turner	2004					
6	Librarian of the Year	Sally Smith	2005					
7	Librarian of the Year	Melody Music	2006					
8	Librarian of the Year	Harry Potter	2007					
9	Librarian of the Year	Sally Smith	2008					
10	Librarian of the Year	Tim Burr	2009					
11	Librarian of the Year	Max Power	2010					
12	Librarian of the Year	Pearl Button	2011					
13	Librarian of the Year	Lily Pond	2012					
14	Librarian of the Year	Sally Smith	2013					
15	Innovation Award	Sally Smith	2013					
16	Librarian of the Year	Lucy Fur	2014					
17	Innovation Award	Holly Day	2014					
18	Librarian of the Year	Heidi Clare	2015					
19	Innovation Award	Jo King	2015					
20								

In the first formula, the COUNTIF statement looks through the range B2 to B19, and counts the number of entries that are equal to "Sally Smith." The second formula does the same thing, but instead of typing in "Sally Smith," I have pointed the formula to the value in cell E3, which happens to be "Sally Smith." If I pointed it to cell B4, the formula would have returned an answer of 1, as there is only one "Ellie Vader" in the list.

The formulas in cells G2 and G3 have the same structure, its just a slightly different way of doing things. Usually, its better to refer to a cell, than to plug the actual value into a formula. This is because if I changed the spelling of "Sally Smith" to "Sally Smyth," then I would need to update the formula, as well as all the cells.

The third formula uses COUNTIFS, and is only available in more recent versions of Excel. It has the same functionality as the above formula, with the only difference being that you can run multiple criteria. In the above example, Sally received four awards all up, of which three were "Librarian of the Year," and one was the "Innovation Award." If you wanted to count the number of times Sally received the Librarian of the Year award, then you would need to use the COUNTIFS formula.

The formula is = COUNTIFS(B2:B19, H4, A2:A19, I4).

If you find that too confusing, then refer to this formula instead: = COUNTIFS (B2:B19, "Sally Smith," A2:A19, "Librarian of the Year").

The first part of this formula starts of the same as the regular COUNTIF formula – i.e., the formula looks through the list of names and counts the number of times it finds the name "Sally Smith." The second part of the formula (i.e., ...A2:A19, "Librarian of the Year") looks through the range A2 to A19, and counts the number of "Librarian of the Year" entries. The formula then only returns those rows where both those criteria are satisfied. There are only three rows where the Staff Name is "Sally Smith," and the Award Name is "Librarian of the Year," so the formula returns 3.

If you have Excel 2003, and need this formula, don't panic. There is almost always more than one way to do something in Excel. For example, you could use SUMPRODUCT:

	A	B	C	D	E	F	G	H
1	Award Name	Staff name	Year					
2	Librarian of the Year	Gail Force	2001				=COUNTIF(B2:B19, "Sally Smith")	=4
3	Librarian of the Year	Darth Vader	2002		Sally Smith		=COUNTIF(B2:B19,E3)	=4
4	Librarian of the Year	Ellie Vader	2003		Sally Smith	Librarian of the Year	=COUNTIFS(B2:B19, E4, A2:A19, F4)	=3
5	Librarian of the Year	Paige Turner	2004					
6	Librarian of the Year	Sally Smith	2005					
7	Librarian of the Year	Melody Music	2006				=SUMPRODUCT(--(A2:A19=F4), --(B2:B19=E4))	=3
8	Librarian of the Year	Harry Potter	2007					
9	Librarian of the Year	Sally Smith	2008					
10	Librarian of the Year	Tim Burr	2009					
11	Librarian of the Year	Max Power	2010					
12	Librarian of the Year	Pearl Button	2011					
13	Librarian of the Year	Lily Pond	2012					
14	Librarian of the Year	Sally Smith	2013					
15	Innovation Award	Sally Smith	2013					
16	Librarian of the Year	Lucy Fur	2014					
17	Innovation Award	Holly Day	2014					
18	Librarian of the Year	Heidi Clare	2015					
19	Innovation Award	Jo King	2015					
20								

The formula SUMPRODUCT might look a bit intimidating at first, but its not that bad. The formula I used was:

= SUMPRODUCT(--(A2:A19 = F4), --(B2:B19 = E4))

Alternatively, if you find " =F4" and " =E4" confusing, refer to this formula instead:

= SUMPRODUCT(--(A2:A19 = "Librarian of the Year"), --(B2:B19 = "Sally Smith"))

SUMPRODUCT sums the values in a range (array), depending upon the criteria you applied. Just like the COUNTIFS formula, you can use multiple criteria. The double -- after the first bracket forces Excel to treat true and false as 1 and 0. So what the hell does this mean?? Well, the first part of the formula looks in the range (array) A2 to A19 for any cell that contains "Librarian of the Year" (remember, F4 contains the text "Librarian of the Year," we could have used that text instead of F4 if we wanted). Now, every time that the formula finds "Librarian of the Year" it returns a value of TRUE. So, its just like you running your finger down the list and asking, is that a Librarian of the Year award, and then answering true or false, depending upon what is actually in the cell. You cannot add up TRUEs, so putting the "--" in the formula forces Excel to convert all the trues to 1s and falses to 0.

So, imagine now you are running your finger down the list of awards, and every time you see "Librarian of the Year" you write down 1. If you summed all those 1s up, you would get 15, and this is exactly what this formula would return if it stopped at that point. However, there is a second part to the formula "--(B2:B19 = E4)." This second part of the formula follows the same logic as the first part. If you were to do this manually, you would scan your finger down the list of staff names, and every time you found Sally Smith you would add 1 to your note pad. If you were only counting Sally Smiths you would get 4. But you are not. The formula is counting each row where the award is "Librarian of the Year" AND the recipient is "Sally Smith." There are only three rows that fit that criteria, so hence the answer is 3.

As I said previously, there are always more ways to do things in Excel, though some are unnecessarily complex. Here is another way to count the number of times Sally Smith won the "Librarian of the Year" award. The following example is probably too complex in this context:

	A	B	C	D	E	F	G	H	I		
1	Award Name	Staff name	Year	Concatenation							
2	Librarian of the Year	Gail Force	2001	=A2&B2		= Librarian of the YearGail Force				=COUNTIF(B2:B19, "Sally Smith")	= 4
3	Librarian of the Year	Darth Vader	2002	=A3&B3		= Librarian of the YearDarth Vader	Sally Smith			=COUNTIF(B2:B19,H3)	= 4
4	Librarian of the Year	Ellie Vader	2003	=A4&B4		= Librarian of the YearEllie Vader	Sally Smith	Librarian of the Year		=COUNTIFS(B2:B19, H4, A2:A19, I4)	= 3
5	Librarian of the Year	Paige Turner	2004	=A5&B5		= Librarian of the YearPaige Turner					
6	Librarian of the Year	Sally Smith	2005	=A6&B6		= Librarian of the YearSally Smith					
7	Librarian of the Year	Melody Music	2006	=A7&B7		= Librarian of the YearMelody Music					
8	Librarian of the Year	Harry Potter	2007	=A8&B8		= Librarian of the YearHarry Potter				=SUMPRODUCT(--(A2:A19=H4), --(B2:B19=H4))	= 3
9	Librarian of the Year	Sally Smith	2008	=A9&B9		= Librarian of the YearSally Smith					
10	Librarian of the Year	Tim Burr	2009	=A10&B10		= Librarian of the YearTim Burr			Librarian of the YearSally Smith	=COUNTIF(D2:D19, I9)	= 3
11	Librarian of the Year	Max Power	2010	=A11&B11		= Librarian of the YearMax Power					
12	Librarian of the Year	Pearl Button	2011	=A12&B12		= Librarian of the YearPearl Button					
13	Librarian of the Year	Lily Pond	2012	=A13&B13		= Librarian of the YearLily Pond					
14	Librarian of the Year	Sally Smith	2013	=A14&B14		= Librarian of the YearSally Smith					
15	Innovation Award	Sally Smith	2013	=A15&B15		= Innovation AwardSally Smith					
16	Librarian of the Year	Lucy Fur	2014	=A16&B16		= Librarian of the YearLucy Fur					
17	Innovation Award	Holly Day	2014	=A17&B17		= Innovation AwardHolly Day					
18	Librarian of the Year	Heidi Clare	2015	=A18&B18		= Librarian of the YearHeidi Clare					
19	Innovation Award	Jo King	2015	=A19&B19		= Innovation AwardJo King					

In this example, I added a field called "Concatenation," which is a fancy word for join, in column D. Under this heading I added a formula that combined the text of "Award Name" with "Staff Name" into a single cell. I then used COUNTIF to count the number of rows in column D that contained the text "Librarian of the YearSally Smith."

CONCATENATE. Even though the above formulas are unnecessary, as there is a much simpler formula available for the required job, there are times when you will need to create a combined key, or simply join values. Say you have a list of first names, and surnames, and you wanted the full name. You can do this one of two ways:

	A	B	C	D	E	F
1	First name	Surname	Full name	Full name		
2	Lucy	Fur	=A2 & " " & B2	=CONCATENATE(A2, " ", B2)		= Lucy Fur
3	Holly	Day	=A3 & " " & B3	=CONCATENATE(A3, " ", B3)		= Holly Day
4	Heidi	Clare	=A4 & " " & B4	=CONCATENATE(A4, " ", B4)		= Heidi Clare
5	Jo	King	=A5 & " " & B5	=CONCATENATE(A5, " ", B5)		= Jo King
6						

Both the formulas in columns C and D return the same result. I prefer the formula in column C, because its shorter. But that is just a personal preference.

SUMIF. The best way to think of SUMIF is as a COUNTIF that sums up the values, rather than count them. However, if you have skipped COUNTIF, or are still struggling a bit with it, you probably would be annoyed with me referring you back to COUNTIF. So, here is a SUMIF example.

	A	B	C	D	E	F	G	
1	Date	Sensor name	Visits	Library Buiding				
2	1-Feb-15	W01	1024	Main				
3	2-Feb-15	W01	1169	Main			=SUMIF(D:D, "Main",C:C)	= 9016
4	3-Feb-15	W01	1178	Main		Main	=SUMIF(D2:D13, F4, C2:C13)	= 9016
5	4-Feb-15	W01	1187	Main				
6	1-Feb-15	W02	1019	Main				
7	2-Feb-15	W02	1182	Main				
8	3-Feb-15	W02	1058	Main				
9	4-Feb-15	W02	1199	Main				
10	1-Feb-15	Z01	107	Smallsville				
11	2-Feb-15	Z01	113	Smallsville				
12	3-Feb-15	Z01	162	Smallsville				
13	4-Feb-15	Z01	184	Smallsville				
14								

There are two versions of the SUMIF formula here, and both are doing the same job, they are just structured slightly differently. SUMIF adds all the values in a specified range, but only if the cells in corresponding range meet your criteria. For example, say you wanted to total up all the visits to the main library, and you wanted to do this manually. You would scan your eye down column D, and every time you saw the word "Main," you would look at the corresponding row in column C, and write down that number on a separate piece of paper. Then once you have finished scanning the list, you would get your piece of paper, and add up all the numbers. SUMIF is doing the same thing. In the first example (the formula in cell G3), SUMIF looks through the range D:D, and looks for the word "Main." When the formula finds the word "Main," it looks across to corresponding row in column C, and adds that to a running total. So, when the formula looks at cell D2, it sees that the contents of the cell is "Main," so it takes the number 1024 in cell C2, and adds it to a running total.

The syntax for the SUMIF formula is: SUMIF(range, criteria, sum range). So the first part of the formula points to the range containing your criteria (e.g., the Library Building name in column D). The second part of the formula, "criteria," specifies the criteria you wish to apply, e.g., we are only interested in the "Main" library. The last part of the formula, "sum range," points to the range that contains the values you want to sum when your criteria are meet, which in this case is column C.

VLOOKUP. If SUM is the bread of Excel formulas, then VLOOKUP is the butter. They are unavoidable, and you will have to use them at some point in your formula writing career. The VLOOKUP formula is like the index in a book, it helps you to find something. Imagine you had a spreadsheet that contained the number of library visits, and that you populated this spreadsheet by exporting data from your gate sensor software. Imagine that you were able to export three fields, the date, the sensor name and the number of visits. Each senor has a unique name. You have two entry gates for your Main Library, and the sensors for these are named W01 and W02. You also have a smaller satellite library located, naturally enough, in the quiet suburb called "Smallsville." The sensor at Smallsville is called "Z01."

When you are asked to report on the number of visits, you are not going to report how many visits there were for W01, W02, and Z01. Your audience would be confused, and even if they did understand what the codes meant, they would most likely not be interested in your data being broken down by the two sensors for the Main Library. Chances are they are only going to want to know how many visits there were by location at best. If we are using pivot tables, and we absolutely should be (discussed in Chapter 7), then you must also have another column that summarizes the sensor names by library building. You could do this manually, i.e., type in the library building for each and every record:

⊿	A	B	C	D
1	Date	Sensor name	Visits	Library Buiding
2	1-Feb-15	W01	1024	Main
3	2-Feb-15	W01	1169	Main
4	3-Feb-15	W01	1178	Main
5	4-Feb-15	W01	1187	Main
6	1-Feb-15	W02	1019	Main
7	2-Feb-15	W02	1182	Main
8	3-Feb-15	W02	1058	Main
9	4-Feb-15	W02	1199	Main
10	1-Feb-15	Z01	107	Smallsville
11	2-Feb-15	Z01	113	Smallsville
12	3-Feb-15	Z01	162	Smallsville
13	4-Feb-15	Z01	184	Smallsville

Here there are only 13 rows of data, so its not such a big job. However, if you have tens of thousands of rows of data, which is quite probable if you can export your data by the hour, then no sane person would suggest you type this in manually. This is where VLOOKUP steps in. If W01 always represented the main library, W02 always represented the main library, and Z01 always represented Smallsville, then wouldn't it be wonderful if there was a formula that we could use to look up this value in a table, and tell us what library building the sensor belongs to. This is what VLOOKUP does. Below is our lookup table for the job, it tells us the name of each gate sensor, and the library building the sensor is located in.

Sensor name	Library Buiding
W01	Main
W02	Main
Z01	Smallsville

All the VLOOKUP formula needs to do then is to use the sensor name in our main table, and return the corresponding Library Building name. It's a bit like being given a key to a post office box. Once you have the post office box number, you can go off and retrieve the contents of the post office box.

	A	B	C	D	E	F	G	H
1	Date	Sensor name	Visits	Library Buiding			Sensor name	Library Buiding
2	1-Feb-15	W01	1024	=VLOOKUP(B2, G2:H4, 2, FALSE)			W01	Main
3	2-Feb-15	W01	1169				W02	Main
4	3-Feb-15	W01	1178				Z01	Smallsville
5	4-Feb-15	W01	1187					
6	1-Feb-15	W02	1019					
7	2-Feb-15	W02	1182					
8	3-Feb-15	W02	1058					
9	4-Feb-15	W02	1199					
10	1-Feb-15	Z01	107					
11	2-Feb-15	Z01	113					
12	3-Feb-15	Z01	162					
13	4-Feb-15	Z01	184					

This is the formula: =VLOOKUP(B2, G2:H4, 2, false). The syntax for VLOOKUP is:

VLOOKUP(lookup value, table array, column index number, [range lookup – i.e., approximate or exact match]).

Here is how it works. The first part of the formula, "B2," is the value you are looking up. If you look in cell B2, you will see that the value being looked up is "W01." "W01" is the equivalent of your post office box number. The second part of the formula "G2:H4", says "here is where you are looking for the data". This is the equivalent of the Post Office address. The third part of the formula, "2" says "what we are looking for is in the second column." The second column of what? The second column of the range you told it to look in, i.e., G2:H4. Therefore, column H is the second column. Finally the last part of the formula "false," says "only return something that matches the lookup value ('W01') exactly." So, this formula is looking for "W01" in column G, and if it finds and exact match, which it does, return the corresponding value in the second column of the lookup table (column H). So the formula in D2 returns "Main."

If you are still struggling with this, imagine you had to manually enter the library building into the spreadsheet. You would look at the sensor name, scan your eyes across to the sensor table, look for W01 in that table, and then when you found it, you would know what library building the sensor was located in by scanning your eyes across to the cell on the right. The VLOOKUP formula is doing exactly the same thing.

You might notice that VLOOKUP does not specify which column in the range G2:H4 to look for "W01." This is because VLOOKUP always looks in the first column of the "table array," which in this case is column G. So if you swapped columns G and H around, the formula would no longer work.

The lookup table can be located anywhere, on any worksheet, or even in another workbook (not advised!). In this case I have put the lookup table on the same sheet in range G2 to H4, so you can see it easily. Normally, however, you would put it on another sheet. Notice I have used relative addressing in the above formula, which means when I fill it down to row 13, only the first formula will have the correct address for the lookup table. Try copying this example, and filling the formula in cell D2 down to D13, you will see what I mean. The simple answer is to use absolute addressing for the lookup table by using the $ sign as follows: =VLOOKUP(B2, $G$2:$H$4, 2, FALSE). This will ensure that as you paste the formula down, it will keep pointing correctly to the lookup table, which does not move.

HLOOKUP. This formula is like the poor neglected cousin of VLOOKUP, except in this case, you probably should keep HLOOKUP locked up in the attic, and only let out in the sun on the rare occasion. The best way to imagine HLOOKUP, is to understand VLOOKUP, then rotate your head 90° to the horizontal position. It does exactly the same as VLOOKUP, but only horizontally. The reason I say you should use it very rarely is because if you have structured your tables correctly, they will be in columns, and therefore any lookups you require will be in the vertical, not the horizontal axis.

Named ranges. These are a fantastic tool for making your spreadsheet easier to understand and manage. When you write a formula, you can address the cell directly, use indirect referencing, or use a named range. For example, with the visits spreadsheet, we could put the sensor lookup table on a new sheet, define the lookup table as a named range, then you could use that named range in the VLOOKUP formula. There is a chance that did not make much sense, so here is the step-by-step version. If you have not already done so, go back and read the VLOOKUP formula above before reading on.

Firstly, put your lookup tables on a sheet called "Validation." Next, you will need to use the name manager. This will be located in different places, depending upon the version of Excel you are running. So, you might have to do a little detective work via the built-in help or Google to find it. Once you have found how to activate the name manager, the next step it is to use it. Highlight the lookup table (G6 to I8 below), then call it a sensible name. A sensible name is one that will make sense in the formula, i.e., it is brief and reasonably self-explanatory.

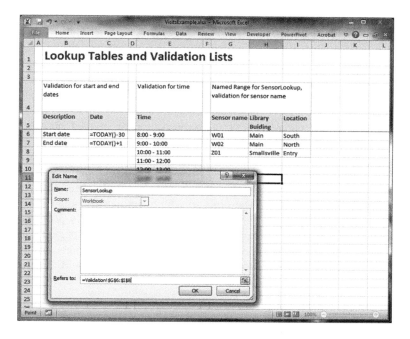

I have called this range "SensorLookup." Notice how Excel defaults to using absolute addresses (the $ signs) for the address. This is good; we want it to be absolute. The named ranges have a horrible habit of radically shifting position when you add and delete columns and/or rows. Using absolute addresses (i.e., using the $ symbol), stops this behavior. So if it is not an absolute address, make it one. When you click OK, you will now have a new named range called "SensorLookup." You can type this in the same way you would have previously used the range "G6:I8". For example, if you wanted to simplify your previous formula for looking up the building a sensor is located in, you could now change your formula to: = VLOOKUP(B2, SensorLookup, 2, FALSE)

◢	A	B	C	D	E
1	Date	Sensor name	Visits	Library Buiding	
2	1-Feb-15	W01	1024	=VLOOKUP(B2, SensorLookup, 2, FALSE)	
3	2-Feb-15	W01	1169		
4	3-Feb-15	W01	1178		
5	4-Feb-15	W01	1187		
6	1-Feb-15	W02	1019		
7	2-Feb-15	W02	1182		
8	3-Feb-15	W02	1058		
9	4-Feb-15	W02	1199		
10	1-Feb-15	Z01	107		
11	2-Feb-15	Z01	113		
12	3-Feb-15	Z01	162		
13	4-Feb-15	Z01	184		
14					

Not only is this tidier and easier to read, but it also has other advantages. If your library expands, and you open a new building, you only have to remember to update the sensor lookup table, and ensure that the named range is updated accordingly. Any formula that refers to the SensorLookup named range would be automatically updated. So it also makes managing the data easier.

This is the vanilla version. You can also use a dynamic named range, one that will automatically expand and contract when you add or delete new values to a list. That way, if you need to add values to a lookup table, you do not even need to worry about updating the named range — as it will happen automatically.

Dynamic named ranges. When you go to edit a named range, and you click on the formula, it will highlight the cells to which the named range refers. This is a good way for checking whether your named range is actually pointing to the right cells. If the dashed line is not highlighting what you expected, then you need to adjust your formula. I have used a dynamic named range in the below screenshot. If I added a new sensor into row 9, the formula would automatically expand to accommodate the new data.

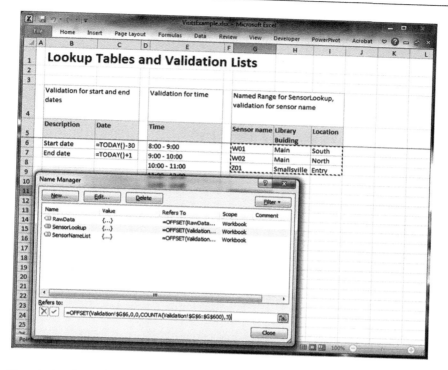

Here is the formula and how it works:

=OFFSET(Validation!$G$6,0,0, COUNTA (Validation!$G$6:$G$600), 2)

The OFFSET function returns a cell or range from another place in the workbook. This will not make much sense at the first, so just continue to plough through for a bit longer.

The OFFSET formula structure is OFFSET(reference, rows, columns, [height], [width]). Wherever you see [ ] in Excel, that means these values (arguments) are optional — i.e., you could end the formula at "columns".

The first part of the formula, the "reference" section, is your starting point. In our case the starting point is cell G6. This is because regardless of how many sensors I add to the list, the first sensor in this particular sheet will always be located in cell G6. Therefore that is our starting point. The word "Validation!" in front of G6 is simply the name of the worksheet. Since we are working across several worksheets, we need to know which sheet we are pointing to. The next part of the formula is the number of rows and columns we want to offset. In this instance, we don't want to use those functions, so we plug in zero for rows, and zero for columns. If we plugged in a value of one for rows and one for columns, the range would not start at G6, it would start at H7. And this is not what we want in this case. See how plugging a 1 into the rows and columns moved the dashed line across so as that the starting point is now at H7. The dashed line covers the range that our formula refers to, and while in some situations we might want to offset our range by a certain number of rows and columns, this is not one of them. Consequently, I have plugged zero into the row and column values for the formula.

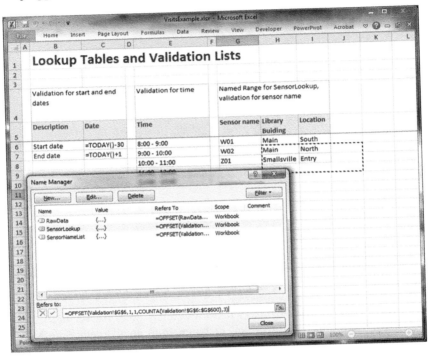

What we do want to do, however, is make the formula refer to a range that will cover all the sensors we might wish to add to the list. The last part of the formula, the 2 at the end, is the easiest. We will always have two columns for this data, the "Sensor Name," and the "Library Building." Consequently, the range width will always be 2. The last part of the formula refers to the cell width: OFFSET(reference, rows, columns, [height], [**width**]), so that is why the number 2 is at the end. The [height] section of the formula is the most tricky, as this will change as we add or delete sensors to the list. The best way to know how many values there are in the list is to count them, and that is exactly what I have done. COUNTA counts all the cells that are not blank within a specified range. I have asked the formula to count all the non-blank cells between G6 and G600. I chose G6 as the starting point, as there should always be a value in G6. The reason I selected G600, however, was arbitrary. I could not count the cells between G6 and G7, because in this example there is a value in A8. If I did this, the formula would not capture the full range, as there are only two non-blank cells between G6 and G7, but there are three rows of data. Consequently I picked 600, because I thought the list would never extend beyond the row 600, so it was pretty safe to count non-blanks between the range G6 to G600. If your list ever did grow past row 600, then you would need to change this formula. So always try to imagine the most outrageous list possible, then double it to be safe.

As you can see, a formula that looks quite complex is actually very simple when broken down into its component parts. Using a dynamic named range may seem like a lot of unnecessary work, but I assure you, that is not the case. A good spreadsheet is robust and flexible. You will inevitably change lookups and validation lists, and if you don't ensure that your named ranges are automatically capturing these changes, then you will have to do this manually. This will be a big job if you have a lot of lookups and validation lists. Worse still, if the ranges for lookups and validations are not automatically adjusted, then when you update those lists, there is a good chance you will forget to update the static ranges your lists are using. The amount of time it takes to create dynamic named ranges is only marginally longer than it takes to make a static one, and the first time you have to update the list, those seconds you saved by using a static list will be immediately lost. So don't be lazy, keep re-reading this section on dynamic named ranges until you understand them, then use them.

Typical error messages and what they mean

At some point in your formula writing career, Excel is going to give you some cryptic looking error messages. It is important that you know why you have an error, if you wish to address that error.

Here are the error messages you are most likely to encounter, and what they mean

1. **#######** – your columns are not wide enough. Excel cannot work miracles. If you make the columns narrower than the values contained in them, then sometimes it will not be able to show you anything sensible. When this happens Excel will show ####### in the cell. The solution, make your column wider.
2. **#DIV/0!** – you cannot divide something by zero, if you try it you will get this error.
3. **#N/A** – Excel cannot find a value to put in the cell. For example, if I asked VLOOKUP to find a value that did not exist, such as a gate sensor named "Q," then the formula would return "#N/A." If I added Q to my SensorLookup table, then that error message would go away. This error message is one of the more important ones to remember, as it is tells you that your lookup tables are incomplete.
4. **#NAME?** – you have made a typo! If you spell a formula name incorrectly, then you will get the error message "#NAME?" On some versions of Excel, and little icon will pop up (in this case an explanation mark) which you can click on to get more information about the error.
5. **#REF!** – you will get this error if you deleted the rows or columns that the formula was relying upon. For example, if I had a formula that added A1 to A2, then I deleted row 2, the formula no longer knows what it should be adding, as you deleted one of the rows it

was referring to. So, in this instance the formula will return a #REF! error. This error can also happen if cells are dragged and dropped over formulas.

6. **#VALUE!** — you have tried to add things that cannot be added, like in the below example, 1024 + "Main" = nonsense.

Managing error messages

There are situations where it might be impossible to avoid an error, but you don't want users to see an ugly error message that might just confuse and worry them. So long as you know exactly why you are getting the error message, and in that context it is perfectly OK to ignore the error, then you can use a formula to do something different if an error is found. For example, say you wanted to allow users to add new sensor codes to the raw data sheet for visits, but you also wanted to let the user know if they have added a code that is not in your lookup table. You could do something like this:

	A	B	C	D
1	Date	Sensor name	Visits	Library Buiding
2	1-Feb-15	Q	1024	=IFERROR(VLOOKUP(B2,SensorLookup,2,FALSE),B2&" not found in Sensor Lookup table")

And this is what the formula returns:

	A	B	C	D
1	Date	Sensor name	Visits	Library Buiding
2	1-Feb-15	Q	1024	Q not found in Sensor Lookup table
3	2-Feb-15	W01	1169	Main
4	3-Feb-15	W01	1178	Main
5	4-Feb-15	W01	1187	Main
6	1-Feb-15	W02	1019	Main
7	2-Feb-15	W02	1182	Main
8	3-Feb-15	W02	1058	Main
9	4-Feb-15	W02	1199	Main
10	1-Feb-15	Z01	107	Smallsville
11	2-Feb-15	Z01	113	Smallsville
12	3-Feb-15	Z01	162	Smallsville
13	4-Feb-15	Z01	184	Smallsville

You might not like that error message, no big deal, you change it to whatever you want, like say "unknown."

The formula is: = IFERROR(VLOOKUP(B2, SensorLookup, 2, FALSE), B2&"not found in Sensor Lookup table").

This formula looks long, because it is joining two different formulas. However, if you look at each formula in isolation, it will be much easier to understand. The formula structure for IFERROR is: IFERROR(value, value if error). The IFERROR formula is doing two things, it tests whether an error exists, and if one does not, then it will run whatever formula or value you plug into the first section of the formula (i.e., the "value" section). If there is an error, the formula will return whatever formula or value you plug into the second section of the formula (i.e., the "value if error" section). So in the above formula the first section is running the VLOOKUP formula (see the VLOOKUP example earlier on). If all goes well, and the VLOOKUP does not return an error, then the IFERROR formula will return the results for that VLOOKUP. However, if the VLOOKUP does result in an error, then the IFERROR formula will return the formula or value specified in the second part of the IFERROR formula. So, in row 2, VLOOKUP returns an error, as the value "Q" does not exist in the sensor lookup table. IFERROR then says, well this formula has an error, so I will follow the alternative set of instructions given to me in the second part of the IFERROR formula, which might be something as simple as returning the word "unknown." I used a formula for the error message, to show that it could be a formula — but it could be straight text. The formula I used was to look in the cell B2, and join whatever you find there to the text "not found in Sensor Lookup table."

IFERROR is not available in all versions of Excel, though there are other similar formulas available that with a little extra work will do the trick. For example, ISERROR will return true for certain errors, so you could test if the error exists using an IF statement, and if the error is not present do the formula, and if there is an error, then throw up a warning message.

Stop, police!

6

If a user can stuff up your spreadsheet, then chances are they will. By and large they will not do this intentionally, but that does not matter. If you do not place boundaries on how staff can use your spreadsheets, they will soon render them useless. With all the effort you are spending on collecting the data, you want to ensure that when it comes time to using the data that it is as accurate and up-to-date as it possibly can be. The bottom line is, data integrity is everything. Without data integrity, all you have is a heap of rubbish numbers. So if you are going to bother collecting the data, then you should do all of the following:

- Store your spreadsheets on a server that is automatically backed up on a daily basis. In most cases your corporate file servers will be backed up, but check if you are unsure.
- Use the workbook, sheet, and cell protection functionality to ensure that staff can only change those parts of your spreadsheets that you want them to change.
- Use data validation wherever possible to ensure that staff can only enter values within a range or from an approved list.
- Create policies and procedures to ensure that data is updated at regular time intervals, and data cannot be retrospectively entered prior to that date.

Protecting data

There are a few levels of protection that apply to spreadsheets:

- You can require users to enter a password to open and/or modify the workbook. You can access this via the "Save as" menu. Look under "Tools" > "General options" on the "Save as" dialog box. Obviously, you should ensure the password is recorded somewhere safe that a few key staff can access. It is highly unlikely that you will need to apply this level of protection, because if you don't want someone else to see something, the simplest solution is to save it to a place that only authorized staff can access.
- You can stop users from moving, hiding, un-hiding, deleting or renaming worksheets by clicking on the "Protect Workbook" icon, and ticking "Protect workbook for structure." You should protect any workbook that will be used by multiple staff. You should also enter a password, because it only takes one person to realize they can do away with the annoying straightjacket you have put on them by simply clicking again on "Unprotect Workbook," and then before you know it, everyone knows, and like a bunch of inquisitive gibbons they all start clicking away the protection, and unconsciously vandalizing your workbooks. Not good!

- Excel allows you to control many aspects of what users can and cannot do with a worksheet. When you click on "Protect Sheet," you will get the following options:

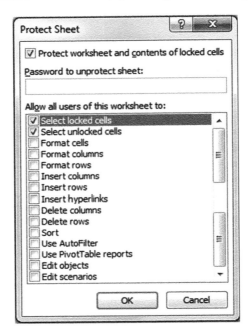

   I am very draconian, and I usually only allow users to select unlocked cells, and use pivot tables. This has turned out to be a very good policy, and one I strongly recommend you go with. When you protect a sheet, the same deal applies. If you don't use a password, then you will soon find that staff will just unprotect your sheet.

If you only want users to select unlocked cells, then you will need to define which cells are locked, and which are not. You will also need to protect the sheet. Anyone can do anything with a locked cell if the sheet has not been protected.

   There are several ways to lock a cell. Most versions of Excel will allow you to right click a cell, select "Format Cells," then select the "Protection" tab on the "Format Cells" dialogue box. Then you tick or untick the "Locked" checkbox.

   Setting up your cell protection is simple if you have organized your data according to the structure outlined in Chapter 5.

- The first step is to make sure all the cells are locked. Click on the square in the top left hand corner of the Excel grid. This action will select all cells. Next, open up the Format Cells dialogue, and select locked. Doing this locks every single cell on the sheet.
- Step two is to unlock all the columns that you are happy for your staff to enter data into. Select all the columns of data under which you are happy for staff to enter data. Don't worry at this point that your selection will include headers. Open Format Cells dialogue, then uncheck the locked check box.

- The final step is to lock the cells above the header. Select every row down to and including the header row, open the Format Cells dialogue, then select locked.

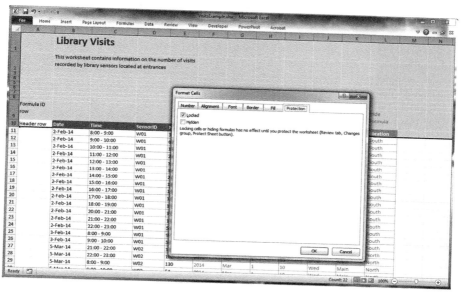

After those three steps you need to protect the sheet. Once this is done, in this example, the only cells that staff will be able to edit are those between columns B and E for rows 11 onwards In this example the formulas are completely safe, the title and the column headers are also completely safe. If you have used data validation, the risk of invalid data will be greatly reduced. You should hide anything the users does not need to see, which in this example is column A, and columns F through to L. This will provide staff with a very clean and easy to use data entry screen.

Data validation

It is still possible for users to muck up your spreadsheet even after you have locked down all the appropriate cells, and protected the workbook and all the worksheets.

A spreadsheet will be useless if users cannot enter data, but if they are allowed to enter the first thing that comes into their head, then you will end up with the following sort of problems:

- Variables that are described and/or spelled many different ways. For example, if you have a spreadsheet to record information literacy classes, and a field to describe the topic taught, the variety of descriptions for a lesson on Boolean searching might include: searching, searches, search, Boolean, Searching Boolean, Boolean searching, Boolean searches, navigating library discovery layer, etc. When you try to run a pivot table containing the distribution of attendances by topics, you are going to get a new row for each and every way your users describe the same topic.

- Users will enter invalid data. For example, say you were running a series of book reading classes for children, and you asked the facilitator to provide feedback on things such as the children's reaction. You might have a specific list of responses you are interested in, such as unfocused, listening intently, actively engaged. If you left the "Behavioral response" field a free text column, you will get a wide variety of responses that do not offer useful information, such as "one child left early."

- Data that is incorrectly entered, leading to formula errors. For example, someone might enter a date that does not exist, such as 33 Jan 2015. Any formulas that refer to that date will return an error. A user might put text in a cell where a number is expected. For example they might enter the number of visits as "nil," instead of 0. This will also create errors.

Applying data validation rules to cells will mean that users can only enter certain values. For example, you can provide users with a drop down box that has a list of values, and stop them entering anything other than what is in that list. You can force users to enter a number within a range. For example, you might only allow users to enter a number between 20 and 100. You can also force users to enter a valid date, and specify that the date they enter is between two dates. For example, you can specify that users can only enter a valid date between 1 Jan 15 and 31 Dec 15. There are a few other options, but you should get the idea by now. To put it succinctly, the purpose of using data validation is to ensure that users enter values in the way you expect them to be entered.

Applying data validation rules is very simple, and there are two ways to do it. "Hardwire" it into the cell, or refer to a list. You should avoid hardwiring data validation lists, unless you are absolutely sure that the values will not change. You can change hardwired lists, it is just fiddly, and because you have to open the validation rules dialogue box to be able to see the validation rules, it can make maintenance of validation lists much more labor intensive than it needs to be. If you have to hardwire the list, you just type the values directly into the validation list dialogue box. For example, for lists choose "list" as a validation type in the validation dialogue box, and then just type in the values, separating each one with a comma, e.g., Jan, Feb, Mar, Apr, May, Jun, Jul, Aug, Sep, Oct, Nov, Dec. In Excel 2010, the data validation menu is on the Data tab on the Excel main menu.

When you are applying data validation to your raw data sheet, the easiest and most effective way to do it is to apply it to the entire column. Once you have finished applying data validation to each column, you can then remove the data validation from the title and headers by selecting rows 1 to 10 in the below example, then open the data validation dialogue box, and selecting "any value." You only need to do this if you have to edit the headers or title, otherwise, you can just leave rows 1 to 10 as is.

Here is a screenshot showing how you could force users to enter a valid date between 1 Jan 15 and 31 Dec 15:

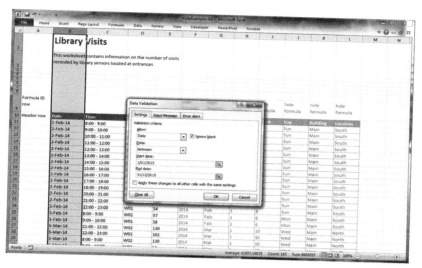

Note that you can type the start and end dates directly in to the Data Validation dialogue box, or you can click on the "select cell" icon on the right hand side of the text box, and point to a specific cell that will contain the start date, and another to contain the end date. This can be useful if you wanted to set your spreadsheet on autopilot. For example, you could point to a cell that contains a formula that makes the start date 30 days before the current day.

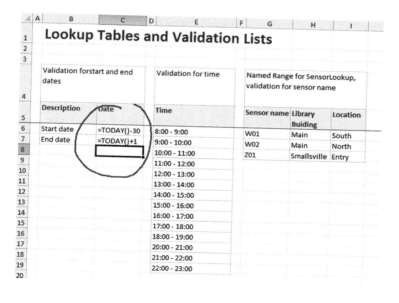

If you pointed the start date in the Data Validation dialogue box to cell $C$6, and the end date to cell $C$7, then the users will only be able to enter a date sometime between 30 days ago, and tomorrow. If you want to use more static start and end dates, then it would still be worth pointing to a cell value, that way you can update all your data validation lists in one place, i.e., the "Validation" sheet.

You may have noticed when you tried using data validation that there are also some other options, including options for specifying input messages, and error alerts. You can use the title and input message to make the data entry a little more user friendly. This is probably of questionable value, but you may find some use in some situations.

The more useful function is the "Error Alert." Using this function you can apply one of three rules. You can stop the user from entering the value, you can give them a warning (which they can ignore), or you can simply provide information. The last two are pretty much the same, they both give the user the option to ignore the data validation rules.

In most cases you are probably going to want to apply the stop rule. However, there might be cases where it is worth being a bit more flexible. For example, staff at your information desk may be required to record the main topic of support they provided. For the most part, the staff might just pick an item from a list. However, you might want to capture the occasional request that does not fall within a predefined list, and allow staff to enter something new after you gave them a warning. This is a good compromise between managing data integrity, and ensuring that you are still able to capture changes in trends. If you are finding that you are getting a lot of new queries, for example, then that in itself will provide you with valuable information that you can use to fine tune your service through training staff to meet these new emerging needs. After a while, you might expand the validation list for the information desk to include these new topics.

While on the topic of lists, the best way to make it easy to manage your validation lists simple is to put them all on the one sheet, and use either a dynamic named range to point to the relevant list, or a table. For example, if you wanted to limit the sensors staff could enter into your visits spreadsheet, then you could do this by creating a dynamic named range called "SensorNameList" (for help with named ranges see previous chapter). The next step is to open the "Data Validation" dialogue box, select "List" from the "Allow" drop down box, then type in "=SensorNameList," without the quotation marks of course!

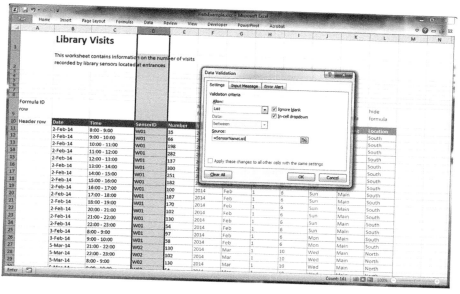

If you have done this correctly, any new sensor you add to your validation list will appear as a new option in your drop down list for sensors.

Dynamic named ranges can scare people, they don't work with dependent lookups, they can start to become a bit unnecessarily complex when using them to drive validation lists (as you might end up with a lot of them), and sorting them can be a little bit fiddly. There is a much better option; using tables. However, I haven't put you through dynamic named ranges just for my own sadistic pleasure, there are many times when you will still need to use them. When it comes to validation lists, however, tables are far superior method for populating validation lists, as they allow you to sort the lists easily.

Using tables

Excel has a function that allows you to convert a range of data into a table. Once a range has been converted to a table, you can easily sort and filter the data by any of your fields. The table automatically expands as you add new rows of data, and when you do this, the table will automatically add any formulas you have in your table to the new row. Finally, you don't have to worry about dynamic named ranges, as any validation list that refers correctly to a table will automatically expand and contract as new data is added or deleted from the table.

Tables sound great, and they are, but there is a good reason for not converting everything to a table. If you use a table, you cannot protect the cells. Well, strictly speaking you can, but that then means the table acts like a range, i.e., you cannot add and delete rows, effectively rendering the table useless as a table. One possible workaround is to not protect your sheet, use validation lists in all the visible columns, and hide any column with a formula. This is quite risky, as there is nothing to stop users changing the field names (which will have an impact on any pivots running off the table), and there is nothing to stop users from deleting formulas accidently from your hidden columns. For these reasons I strongly recommend that you do not use tables for your raw data, at least until Microsoft addresses this Achilles heel for tables.

However, there is no problem using tables for validation lists, as you can put these on a separate worksheet, hide the worksheet, then protect the workbook. The validation lists will be "unprotected," but users will have no way of accessing them unless they have your password to unprotect the workbook.

To insert a table you need to first select the range of cells you wish to convert to a table. Then go to the insert menu, and choose insert table.

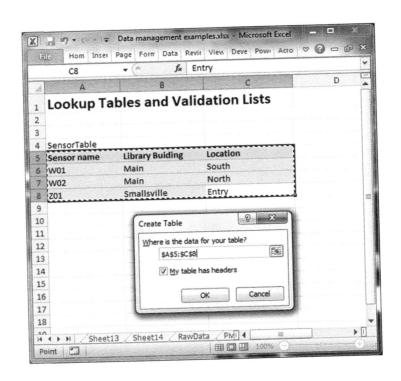

Your table must have headers, as you need to refer to the headers in your formula. The headers should always be in the first row of the table.

After you have inserted a table, you should change its name to something sensible. The default table name will be Table1, then next one will be Table2, etc. Table1 will not be confusing if you only have a few tables. However, if you had say 15 tables, then how are you going to remember what Table11 refers to? You will not remember, so you will spend an inordinate amount of time cross referencing lists, and going back and forth in your spreadsheet. Don't to this, it is just plain silly. Renaming your tables is very easy. The only rule is you cannot use some characters, including spaces.

In Excel 2010 you can rename the table by clicking on the table to activate the table tool menu, then changing the name in the table name box (see arrows):

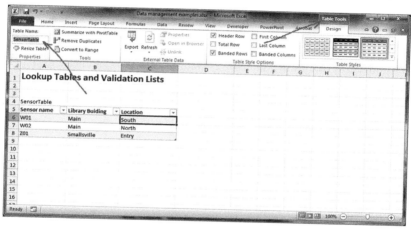

You will notice a few changes after you have converted a range to a table. The table will default to banding format, with alternating blue and white rows. This is just an esthetic thing. The table will have a little dark blue angle (back to front L) at the bottom right row. This is a handle, and you can grab it to manually expand and contract the table. For the most part you will not need to do this, but it can come in handy on rare occasions. Try creating a table now, and practice moving that handle. While you are practicing, try typing a new heading, just to the right of your table. Notice that the table automatically expands to accommodate the new column. Try adding a new bit of data at the end of the table, and hitting enter. Notice that the table automatically expands to accommodate the new row. So tables are dynamic. They will expand as you add new data.

The other dynamic thing about tables is they automatically fill a formula down to the last table row in a column. This means users can add data, and the formulas will be automatically added for those rows. You will also notice that the formula syntax for tables is slightly different. The following is just nonsense data, so as that you can see how the table works without being distracted by real data. I created three headers, "Value 1", "Value 2", and "Sum." After entering four rows of data under "Value 1" and "Value 2" I selected the cells A1 to C5, and inserted a table. Try doing this now yourself. Then click on the cell C2, and type "=" (without the quotation marks of course!), and then click on cell A1, type " + ", then click on cell B2. You will see that the syntax for tables is very different, with the formulas referring to the column headers using "[@[headername]]" format. This is the only thing that is different, all other aspects to crafting formulas remain unchanged. If you build the formula from within the table, by clicking on the cells, Excel will automatically add the field names. You will also notice that when you hit return, the formula will automatically fill down. If you added a value in cell A6, and hit return, you will see the table expands, and the formula is added to C6.

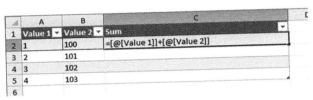

You can delete a row from a table by clicking on a cell, right clicking, and choosing "Delete" > "Table Rows." The wonderful thing is, if you delete a row in this fashion, Excel only deletes the row in the table. Any rows outside the table will not be affected. The same applies to columns.

Finally, you will see that when you create a table the headers all get an inverted triangle icon placed next to them. If you click on this triangle, a menu will pop up for that column header. You can use the menu to sort the list, you can search for values using a range of Boolean type functions, you can do a quick search using the search box, or you can filter using the check box.

Using a table to populate a validation list

To populate a validation list with the contents from a column in a table, the first thing you need to do is to create the table. Once you have done this, select the column in your raw data table to which you wish to apply the data validation. In this example, I am applying data validation to the sensor name for our Library Visits spreadsheet. This will ensure that users cannot make up a sensor name that does not exist, they have to choose a real sensor from a list that I give them.

I created the below table, and named it "SensorTable"

	A	B	C
1	**Lookup Tables and Validation Lists**		
2			
3			
4	SensorTable		
5	Sensor name	Library Buiding	Location
6	W01	Main	South
7	W02	Main	North
8	Z01	Smallsville	Entry
9			

I then went to my raw data sheet, selected column D, activated the Data Validation dialogue box, selected allow list, then entered the following formula: =INDIRECT("SensorTable[Sensor Name]")

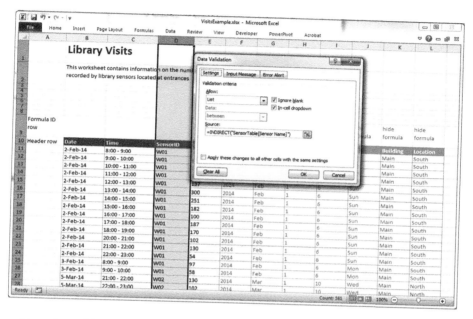

How does this formula work? The INDIRECT formula allows you to indirectly refer to a cell, named range, or range. It's a bit like when you were at school, and you were keen on someone but too scared of being rejected, so you put a friend up to asking that person whether they liked you too. You get the answer, but not directly from the person you are interested in, you get the answer via your friend. The INDIRECT formula does a similar thing. In this example, the size of the SensorTable would change if we added sensors to the table. So we cannot refer to a fixed range, i.e., we cannot hard wire this in directly, as we don't know how big the SensorTable will be in future. This formula in effect is saying, I don't know how big the SensorTable is, so please go off and ask the SensorTable how big it is, then I will use that information to determine how many values I will put into the validation list.

If you are still worried about how the formula works, don't be. All you need to do is plug in the relevant table and header names into the formula.

Dependent lookups

The last type of lookup is a dependent lookup. There might be occasions where you want users to have different values to choose from in the lists, depending upon the information they provided previously. For example, if you are collecting information about the types of help you are providing at various service points, then you would probably want a different list of items staff could help clients with, depending upon the type of help provided by the staff member. A person that provides help at the information desk may answer questions about where to find the toilets, but never be expected to answer questions about where to find information on executives in the car industry.

By far the easiest way to create dynamic dependent lookups is to use tables. Unfortunately, Excel throws a few obstacles in the path of creating dynamic dependent lookups, but there is a work around that is not too complex. Firstly, here is an example in case you do not know what a dependent look up means.

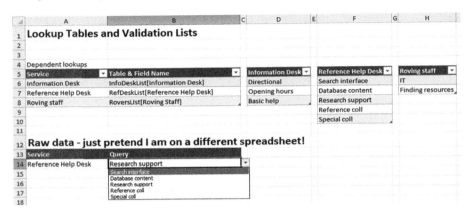

I have committed the sin of putting my raw data on the same sheet as my validation lists, but I only committed this sin so as that you can see the relationship between the dependent lookups and the validation lists more easily. In cell A14 I have selected "Reference Help Desk," which means the values I can select in cell B14 are "Search interface," "Database content," etc. If I changed cell A14 to "Roving staff," then the values I would be able to select in cell B14 would be different, they would be "IT" and "Finding resources." Now please put aside any concerns you might have about the terminology I used, or whether the items in the list are mutually exclusive. It's the concept that counts here, and the concept is that there will be times when you might want to vary the content of a validation list, **depending** upon the value the user selects in another cell. This is why it is called a dependent lookup, the content of one validation list depends upon the value of another cell.

To create a dynamic dependent lookup you need to do the following:

- Define the content of your primary list, and identify what table each value in the list should point to. In the above, for example, the primary list is defined by cells A5 to B8. This table contains a row for each service, and in column B a list of table and field names for the dependent lookup. For example, cell A6 contains the service "Information Desk," and the cell to the right contains the value "InfoDeskList[Information Desk]." "InfoDeskList" is the name of the table starting in cell D5, and "[Information Desk]" is the name of the field (i.e., the column header in cell D5). The primary list table (A5:B8) is used to tell Excel where to find the dependent lookup for any value a user selects in column A of that table.

- Create a dynamic named range for the primary list table. This is a workaround that is necessary to overcome a limitation in the formulas that can be used for validation lists. Because I put the raw data in the same sheet as the validation lists (which you should never do), I had to use a modified version of the formula for which you should now be very familiar: =OFFSET(Validation!$A$6,0,0,COUNTA(Validation!$A$6:$A$11),2). I named this range "ServiceDNR," and named the table occupying cells A5 to B8 "ServiceTable."
- Next you will need to create a separate table for each dependent lookup. These are the three tables starting in cells D5, F5 and H5 – i.e., the tables with the column headers of "Information Desk," "Reference Help Desk," and "Roving Staff," Name these tables something sensible – i.e., a short but intuitive name that follows a consistent naming format. I have named these tables as lists, rather than tables, to reflect the fact that they only have one column. You don't need to do this; you just need to be consistent and meaningful in your name format.
- The next step is to add the data validation to your raw data table. There are two data validation lists you need to add; one for the service, and one for the query. In my raw data sheet, which in this example starts on row 12, I pointed the data validation list for the Service column (i.e., rows A14 down) to the first column in my ServiceTable (i.e., the table occupying cells A5 to B8). I have done this by selecting cell A14, opening the data validation dialogue box, selecting allow list, and inserting the following formula:
   =INDIRECT("ServiceTable[Service]"). This formula asks Excel to retrieve the first column from the ServiceTable (i.e., the [Service] field), and put the values in that field into the validation list. After you do this, you will find when you click in cell A14 that you have a choice to enter one of three values, "Information Desk," "Reference Help Desk," or "Roving Staff." If you added a value to A9, then that would also appear in the validation list for service.
- The final step is to add the dependent lookup for the "Query" column in your raw data sheet. Once again, select cell B14, open the data validation dialogue box, select allow list, and insert the following formula:
   =INDIRECT(VLOOKUP($A14, ServiceDNR, 2, FALSE))
   The VLOOKUP part of the formula gets the value in the cell to the left (e.g., "Reference Help Desk"), then looks for that in the range called "ServiceDNR." It finds the value "Reference Help Desk" in row A7 of that table. The formula then looks for the value in the second column of "ServiceDNR", which happens to be "RefDeskList [Reference Help Desk]." The false bit just means make sure it is an exact match. So "VLOOKUP($A14, ServiceDNR, 2, FALSE)" returns the value 'RefDeskList[Reference Help Desk]." When the VLOOKUP part of the formula is substituted with the value found by VLOOKUP, the formula looks like this =INDIRECT('RefDeskList[Reference Help Desk]"). The INDIRECT formula asks Excel to find the values in the table "RefDeskList", and return all those it finds in that table under the field heading "Reference Help Desk." So in this example, the validation list for cell B14 becomes "Search interface," "Database content," etc.
- To apply the validation list to other cells, simply select a range that includes the cell with the validation, then open the validation dialogue box. Excel will then ask you if you want to extend the validation rules to the other cells, to which you click yes, then OK.

Dynamic dependent lookups are a bit more involved, but once you have done it, you can just set and forget. The only time you will need to fiddle with the formulas is if you add a Service. Once you have written these formulas, you will find them much easier the next time around.

The alternative to using dependent lookups would be to have all the values for each service appear in the validation list. This will become a problem, because it will allow staff to use the data in ways you probably did not intend. For example, as staff member providing roving support might say that they answered a query on research support. If all staff can provide any support, i.e., you have a truly multitasked front line staff, then you will not need dependent lists for this spreadsheet. Otherwise, if you do provide specialized support, then dependent lookups will help to maintain data integrity.

Pivot magic

7

This is the chapter where the threads of everything discussed so far finally start to come together. When I was thinking about the structure of the book I faced a dilemma. On one hand the importance of things such as raw data structure and data validation only make sense when you understand how pivots work. On the other hand, you cannot build functioning pivots unless you know how to structure your raw data properly, and you use data validation. My approach, in the end, was to start from the foundations, and work my way up, and in doing so hoping that the readers would stick with it, understanding that it would be worth it in the end. Once you have started using pivots properly, you will wonder how you ever managed without them.

So, after having made such a fuss about pivots, what is the big deal? Pivots allow you to slice and dice data VERY quickly. They also allow you to present that data in a multitude of ways, and do that very quickly too.

How to create a pivot table

There are only a few steps involved in creating a pivot table:

1. Go to the insert pivot table menu. In Excel 2010, you click on the "Insert" menu, then select the "PivotTable" icon on the far left. This will result in the following dialogue box opening:

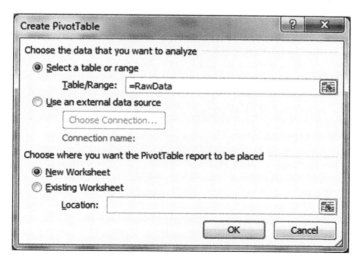

How Libraries Should Manage Data.
© 2016 Brian L. Cox. Published by Elsevier Ltd. All rights reserved.

2. Define the Table/Range the pivot table should cover. You can do this by selecting a range, or using a dynamic named range. Selecting a range is a bad idea. As you add data you want the pivot table to automatically grow to capture this new data. If you select a range, then it will stay fixed to that range, even if you add new data. You can manually extend the range, but firstly it is very easy to forget doing this, and secondly, if you have a lot of pivots, in a lot of spreadsheets, then it will become too time consuming. Hard wiring in the range is lazy and costly. The best option is to use a dynamic named range. This is discussed in the previous chapter, but in case you forgot here is an example of the formula, with each of the bolded parts explained in turn, where the dynamic named range refers to the below raw data for visits:

- =OFFSET(**RawData!**$B$10,0,0,COUNTA(**RawData!**$B$10:$B$60000),11). **RawData!** is the name of the worksheet on which your pivot table is based. As a matter of good practice, all your raw data should be stored in the one range, and all raw data sheets should be called the same name. A sensible name, therefore, is **RawData!**
- =OFFSET(RawData!**$B$10**,0,0,COUNTA(RawData!$B$10:$B$60000),11). **$B$10** is the top left hand cell in your raw data range. In other words, it is your first header, which in this example is "Date."
- =OFFSET(RawData!$B$10,0,0,COUNTA(RawData!**$B$10:$B$60000**),11). **$B$10:$B $60000** is the range of data that the formula will perform a COUNTA on. This formula counts the number of non-blank cells in the range between cells B10 and B60000. The number of non-blank cells counted by the formula will determine how many rows will be captured by the pivot table. For this formula to work there cannot be any blank cells in column B. As a rule there should not be any blank cells anyway, but if there is even a small risk that someone will enter a row of data, and leave column B blank, then you will need to do a count on a different column. Also, if you are expecting to enter more than 60,000 rows of data, you will need to change the 60,000 part of the formula to a larger number.

• =OFFSET(RawData!$B$10,0,0,COUNTA(RawData!$B$10:$B$60000),**11**). **11** is the number of columns of data you want the pivot table to cover. You could make this dynamic too, but it's honestly not worth the effort. Just remember, if you have 11 columns of data, and you add a new column, and you want that column to be captured by the pivot table, you will have to change the "11" in this formula to "12."

All of the above might sound like a lot of work, maybe you think its too much effort. Take my word for it, after you have used this formula once, it will be easy to amend when you create a new pivot table. If you keep your raw data structure consistent, and you should, then the only thing you will most likely need to change after you have used the formula once, is the number of columns (i.e., the number 11 at the end of the above formula). Once you have used a dynamic named range, you have set and can forget your pivot data source.

3. The last step is to choose where you want the pivot table to be placed. This should not be on the raw data sheet. The raw data sheet should be reserved entirely for data entry, for reasons that have already been discussed. The section called "Bringing it altogether" discusses where to place the pivots for maximum impact. For the moment, given you are only practicing, it does not matter where you place the pivot.

Anatomy of a pivot table

After you click OK on the Create PivotTable dialogue box, Excel will create a blank pivot table that will look something like the following:

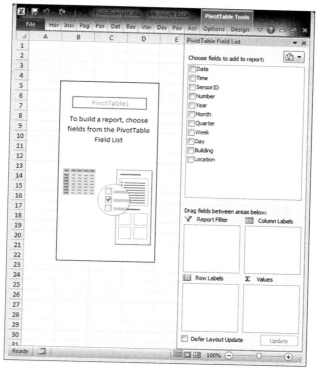

Don't worry about the appearance of the term "fields," they are just your headers. You can drag any of these fields to one of four boxes, Report Filter, Column Labels, Row Labels, and Values. Each of these boxes has a unique function.

- Values – this is what you will be counting, it is the measure. For example, if you wanted to know the size of your collection you could do it several ways. You might count the number of unique titles or you might count the number of items. The values section of the pivot table determines what you are counting, and how you are counting it (e.g., as a count, sum, average, minimum, maximum).
- Column and row labels – this is how you are aggregating your data. For example you might want to know the number of library visits by Month and by library Location. If so, you would drag Month into the Column Labels box, and Location into the Row Labels Box, or vice versa.
- Report filter – this is used to limit the information displayed in the pivot to a subset of data. For example, if you wanted to see library visits by Month and Location, you are probably only going to want to see the data for a specific year. If you drag the Year field into the "Report Filter" box, then you will have the option of filtering down to a specific year.

The pivot table will automatically update as you drag fields into the Report Filter, Column Labels, Row Labels, and Values boxes. The thing you will not see as you build the pivot, is the "Slicer", the box that contains days of the week. Slicers work just like the report filter, except that they are easier to read and change. If you only wanted to see data for visits on Mondays, then you could just click on Monday on the slicer. If you wanted to see data for just Mondays and Thursdays, then you would hold down the control key (Ctrl), and click on Thursday. So slicers allow you to filter data quickly, and you can see what the data is filtered to at a glance. The only cost is that they take up a lot more real estate on your spreadsheet.

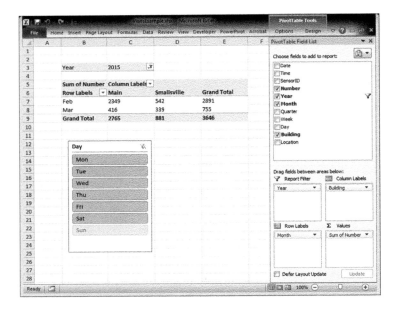

Slicers may not be available in all versions of Excel. To add slicers in Excel 2010 you will need to click on the pivot table to activate the "PivotTable Tools" menu, then under "Options" select the Insert Slicer icon.

You can also filter on multiple items in a Report Filter. For example, click on the inverted triangle next to the Year filter on the pivot table, check the multiple items box, and then select the years you wish to include in the report. You can also use these controls on the Row and Columns fields to filter out items, and to sort the lists.

Bringing it all together

The objective off all of the processes I have encouraged you to follow so far is to create spreadsheets that are robust and easy to use. By robust, I mean that you can depend upon the data. The data will be accurate, up-to-date, and complete. The spreadsheets will be robust for the following reasons:

- They will be easy to use, and therefore they will be used more often, and more likely to be used correctly. They will be easy to use because all your spreadsheets will have a consistent look and feel. If a user is familiar with one sheet, it will not be a big learning curve for them to become familiar with another. I am yet to encounter a type of data that can be managed in a standard spreadsheet that could not be managed using a standardized format. Your spreadsheets will also be easy to use because you will only show users the information they need to see. All the formulas they don't need to see will be hidden. All the sheets they don't need to see will be hidden. Users should only really ever need to see four sheets at most: "RawData" sheet, "Contents" sheet, "Pivot" sheet, and in some cases the "Validation" sheet.
- You will have policies in place supported by lockdown periods to ensure that data is updated by specific dates, such as every quarter.
- You will have strong data validation rules in place to ensure that users can only enter allowable data types.
- You will take the headache out of reporting, giving managers an incentive to support your standardization drive.
- You will make data more accessible, enabling, at the very least, the possibility of turning data into actionable intelligence. If you can achieve this, then you will provide the executive and the managers' further incentive to support standardization.

There are a few last things you need to do before you can say you have created a robust spreadsheet, including setting up the Contents, Pivot, Validation, and RawData sheets.

Set up the Contents sheet

The Contents sheet will allow users to quickly navigate to any "precanned" view you have created. The best way to do this is to create a table number that is completely unique; for example, by combining the acronynm for the spreadsheet with a sequential number. That way when anyone talks about table LV1, you will know that they are refering to Table1 in the Library Visits spreadsheet.

To turn the table number into a hyperlink, right click over the table number cell (e.g., LV1), then click "Hyperlink." There are several things you can link to. Click on "Place in this Document," then click on the "Pivot" sheet, and then add a cell reference. For the first sheet I am linking to cells A1:A51. I will hide column A in the "Pivot" sheet, so as that the user will not see the cells being selected. The purpose of using the range A1:A51 is to ensure that no matter which cell the user had previously activated in the "Pivot" sheet, the user will always be centered on the relevant pivot table when they click on any hyperlink in the "Contents" sheet.

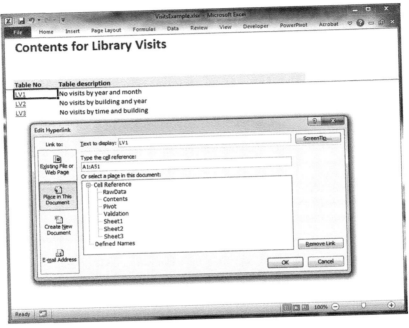

I place all the Pivots on the same sheet, to reduce complexity. However, to do this successfully, you have to make sure that no matter how many rows the Pivot Table occupies, that it will not overwrite another Pivot Table. One Pivot Table cannot overwrite another, so if you have them overlapping, or a refresh causes them to overlap, then an error will occur, and the pivots will not refresh. The simple solution is to take advantage of the large number of rows at your disposal. So I separate all my pivots by a 1000 rows. This means the link for LV2 will be A1000:A1051, and for table LV3, it will be A2000:A2051. It is highly unlikely that you will create a spreadsheet where a user needs 1000 rows in a Pivot Table, so this is a safe approach.

Obviously, you will need to add a table description, and hide things that the user does not need to see in the "Contents" sheet, such as the headers, and the gridlines (via the View menu in Excel 2010). When you have done this you will end up with a nice clean "Contents" page that looks more like a Word document, and should be reasonably self explanatory to all users.

Obviously you can have more tables if you want, and you can always present them in groups of related tables, by, for example, placing related tables underneth each other, and applying the same color shading to those set of tables. Whatever you do, just make it consistent for all your spreadsheets.

Set up the Pivot sheet

Once you have created the "Contents" sheet, and you are sure you have the views you expect most users will want to see, then you can start creating the Pivots for each link on your Contents sheet. First, hide column A in the Pivots sheet. I added the title for the LV1 pivot to cell C2. The purpose of this is so that when I turn off the headers and gridlines, there is a bit of white space above and to the left of the table heading (i.e., row 1 and column B is the white space). This makes it a lot easier for users to read your pivots.

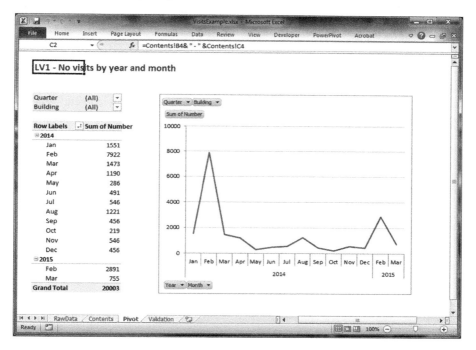

You will also notice that I use a formula to define the pivot title in the above screenshot. That way, if I change a table title on the Contents sheet, it will be automatically updated on the Pivot sheet.

The next step is to insert a pivot table. Remember that you are using a dynamic named range as the Pivot Table data source. Add the pivot at least ten rows down from the title, that way you will have plenty of space to insert your report filters. After you are certain you have included all the report filters you are likely to need, then drag the Pivot Table so as that it starts two rows below the heading, or whatever gap you want, so long as it is consistent.

After you have dragged the relevant fields into the relevant parts of the Pivot Table, you will notice that all the column widths readjust. Personally, I don't like this behavior, and it is problematic when you have all your Pivots starting in the same column. So I prefer to switch this behavior off, by right clicking the Pivot Table, and selecting "PivotTable Options," clicking on the layout and format tab, then deselecting "Autofit column widths on update."

You might also wish to add a chart next to your pivot. To create a PivotChart, click on the Pivot Table to activate it, click on insert, then select a chart. This way, each time a user clicks on a link in your contents page, they will be taken through to a clean and easy to read screen.

Another option I highly recommend you change while you have the PivotTable Options dialogue box open is to show blanks for error values, and on the "Data" tab disable "Enable show details," and enable "Refresh data when opening the file." The latter is self explanatory. You might find it useful to use the "Enable show details" function, but it will only cause confusion for users if they accidently create a drill through report.

Once you have all your pivot table options set, and you are definitely happy with them, I highly recommend that you simply copy the pivot table, then paste it wherever you need another pivot. This will save you having to set the options for each and every pivot.

To insert the other two pivots just follow the same procedure. For example, the heading for LV2 would be entered into cell B1001 (using a formula!), etc. When a user clicks on a link in your contents page it should take them to the relevant pivot.

Set up the RawData sheet

Your RawData sheet should look something like that shown here, with all the information that the users do not need to see hidden:

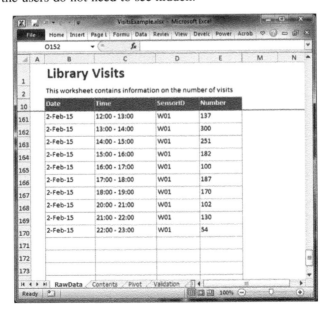

If you use borders for all the rows that have a formula, then it will be obvious when data is being entered in rows without formulas. Once again, the aim is to have a clean and consistent format. You need to have data validation on every single visible column, i.e., data validation for Date, Time, SensorID, and Number. This dramatically reduces the risk that users will enter incorrect data.

These sheets can be a bit tricky for data entry when there is more than one person entering the data. In practice it will be difficult for users to find the last row of data they entered, without scrolling through a long list, and perhaps getting it wrong. The solution to this is to include this data in the spreadsheet.

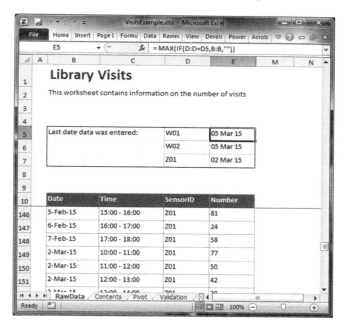

This why it is handy to not have your raw data header start until row 10, as you can squeeze in this sort of information where necessary. If you always keep your header in the same row, that means you can use a script later on to automate much of the work involved in your spreadsheets. It also means you can set up a template.

The formula in the above screenshot has to be entered as an array to work. The way to enter an array formula is to type in the formula, e.g., =MAX(IF(D:D=D6, B:B,"")), then press Ctrl and Shift and Enter. This last action will convert the formula into an array formula. You can't do this simply by typing in the { } characters.

Set up the Validation sheet

In most instances you should be able to hide the Validation sheet from users. However, on the chance that you will need users to be able to change validation lists, then you should set these up consistently too. Here is a screenshot of the Validation sheet for the Library Visits sheet.

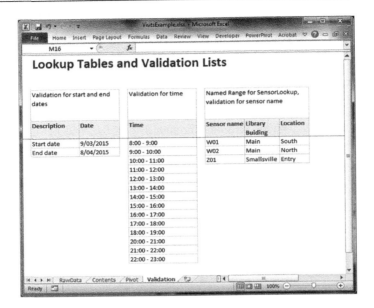

Notice the clean layout, and that information is included above each validation or lookup reference to explain what function the data below it perform. Even if your users do not see this sheet, you should still keep it consistent to make your life easier. If your users do need to update the validation lists, then in might be easier to use tables (see earlier discussion).

Done!

So now you should have a very simple spreadsheet, with only three to four visible sheets. Data entry staff will always know that they can enter data by going to the RawData sheet. Managers will always know they can access their reports via the Contents sheet. And the spreadsheet administrator will always be able to adjust the data validation by accessing the Validation sheet.

If you had your thinking cap on while reading this, you might have realized that you can create a template, save it somewhere safe, and then use that to create any future spreadsheets. Doing this will also ensure that the worksheets are consistent. So do it!

Moving beyond basic pivots

8

Sooner or later you will be faced with serious limitations in what you can do with normal pivot tables. This is where PowerPivot comes to the rescue! PowerPivot performs calculations in a fraction of the time of normal Excel, and it can handle a lot more data. The current version of PowerPivot can handle 1,999,999,997 distinct values in a column, and 1,999,999,997 rows of data. But this is only the tip of what PowerPivot can do.

Before PowerPivot I had written some complex VBA code to produce findings from a large dataset on library usage. I was interested in seeing whether changes in student usage of library resources over the students' years of study correlated with changes in their grades. I found it did, but it took me weeks to get that data, and when I ran the code, I had to run it on a Friday, and when I came to work on the Monday hope that the computer had not crashed, and the code had finished running. I had to solve a problem of similar complexity recently, albeit for a totally unrelated dataset, and when I nutted out the formula I needed, PowerPivot completed the calculation almost instantly. Speed is essential for working on large datasets, life is too short to have to wait a weekend every time you want to run a new calculation. However, speed is no good if it is not backed up by function.

Broadly speaking, PowerPivot provides two additional functions that allow you to perform calculations that would otherwise be impossible using normal pivot tables:

- Formulas that can count distinct items
- Formulas that iterate through every row of data.

While this may not seem very impressive now, the benefit will soon become apparent when you try to use an ordinary pivot table to work with a denormalized table.

A denormalized table is one where you have data that previously existed in a relational database, and it has been exported to a single table. It will include a lot of repetition in the table, i.e., "duplicate" rows. Librarians fully understand resource databases and metadata. You may, however, be a bit rusty on what the structure of a relational database actually encompasses, so to avoid the risk of confusion I will quickly cover this now. Please forgive me if you already know this.

Relational databases

Imagine you were asked to create a system to record two bits of information, the title of a book, and the author. Sounds simple enough. So you create a spreadsheet, and you have one column called "Author," and another called "Title." Your boss then asked you to enter all your books and authors into your new system. The system works fine until you get to the third book. This book has two authors. What do you do? You might decide to rename the second column "Author1," and create a third column called "Author2." Great, you press on. Then you get to the sixth book, which has ten authors! What do you do now? You could continue to press on and create more author columns, but that is not a workable option for two reasons. Firstly, imagine you were asked to produce a list of all the authors. What are you going to do, cut and paste all the author columns into a single column? This would be very time consuming, and error prone. Secondly, imagine that instead of entering books, you were entering data on sales, with one column being the name of the sales person, and another being the name of the customer. A single salesperson might have hundreds, or even thousands of customers. A thousand "customer" columns is unworkable.

The problem is that one book might have many authors. This is called a one-to-many relationship. But it does not stop there. One author might write many books. So when it comes to books, many books can be written by many authors. This is what is called a many-to-many relationship. It is possible to enter such relational data into a single table. However, it comes with many problems. For example, you might decide that you are going to stick with the two columns, one for "Author," and another for "Title," and if a book has two authors, you enter two rows of data. If a book has three authors, you enter three rows of data. And so on...

Author	Title
Joe Bloggs	Why Libraries are great
Jane Smith	Why Libraries are great
Sam Stone	Life of Turtles
Wendy Lane	Libraries of the 22nd century
Joe Bloggs	Libraries of the 22nd century

There is a lot of duplicate data entry, but its not too bad. But what happens if you wanted to also include more information, such as publisher, year of publication, ISBN, etc. The amount of duplicated data entry would soon escalate out of control. What happens if someone enters one of those duplicate entries incorrectly? For a start, any report you run of such a system will be inaccurate. If you used this system to count to count the number of titles by counting the unique ISBNs, then how accurate is your data going to be if many of these have been entered incorrectly? Of course, it is always possible to enter something incorrectly, but the point is such a system is designed so as that mistakes will be almost certain. You want the chances of mistakes to be unlikely, not almost certain. Finally, say you realized that Jane Smith had been entered incorrectly, and it should have been Janet Smith. How are you going to fix this in such a system? Whatever you do it is going to be risky, labor intensive, or both.

For all these reasons, a flat file (i.e., a single table), is a pretty poor tool for entering anything but simple data. Relational databases were created to manage data that consists of many-to-many relationships. Relational databases solve this problem of the many-to-many relationships by splitting the data into separate tables, and creating a joining table.

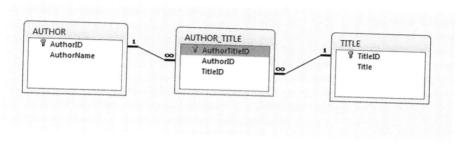

All the authors are entered into the author table, and they are only entered once. That way, if you needed to change Jane Smith to Janet Smith, then you would only need to do it once, in the Author table. In exactly the same vein, all the book titles are entered into the "Title" table, and they are only entered once. You will notice that both the Author and the Title tables have a unique identification field, called AuthorID, and TitleID respectively, and a little key symbol next to them. Given that the author should only be in the database once, you could in this example use the AuthorName as the primary key. However, this is not good practice. What would happen, for example, if we had two authors with the same name? The purpose of the primary key is to uniquely identify each row of data in a table. A lot of databases use sequential numbers that are automatically generated when a user adds a new record. So, in this example, if the first author I entered was "Joe Bloggs," the Joe would get an AuthorID of 1A. If I then entered Jane Smith, she would get an AuthorID of 2A. The order authors are entered is completely irrelevant, and does not matter. The point is once an author is assigned an ID, that ID becomes their ID for the life of the database. It a bit like when new client joins up your library, they are given a number, and that number is their library number, and no one else has that number. The same logic applies to the Title table.

The AUTHOR_TITLE table is where the magic happens. This table can then be used to assign a title to each author, and an author to each title. So, for example if the TitleID for the work "Libraries are great" was 1T, and the AuthorID for Joe Bloggs was 1A, and for Jane Smith her AuthorID was 2A, then your AUTHOR_TITLE table would look like this:

AuthorTitleID	AuthorID	TitleID
1	1A	1T
2	2A	1T

Now, relational databases are fantastic when it comes to entering data. They dramatically reduce the amount of data entry required, the risk of error, and data storage size requirements. However, while relational databases are essential for managing data entry, they can be awful when it comes to data reporting.

Imagine you wanted to produce a report that showed all the titles in your library, and their authors. You could not use the AUTHOR_TITLE, as it would just return nonsense. Don't let the fact that in this very simplistic example we could have used actual author and title names in this table fool you. Real world relational databases quickly become very complex, and using numbers as primary keys is essential. So, to get a report that included data that makes sense to humans we would need to tell the computer for each record in the AUTHOR_TITLE table, go off and fetch the AuthorName for the AuthorID from the AUTHOR table — and while you are at it, do the same sort of thing for the titles, then give this data to me in a new table. So when you want to retrieve data from a relational database, there is no avoiding giving the computer complicated instructions on what it needs to do. These instructions are commonly encoded in a language called Structured Query Language, or SQL for short.

Now, you could get someone to write an SQL query to give you the report you need, and many organizations have databases where this is someone's job. However, writing SQL can be quite labor intensive. If I wanted another report, but this time including publisher details, then the SQL query would need to be amended. In this example it would be relatively straight forward to extend the SQL query, but in many cases it will not, because it will require data to be drawn from across new many-to-many relationships that the previous SQL did not have to worry about.

This is why data warehousing became popular. SQL still plays a role, but a data warehouse can be created to deliver a system where users can build the reports they need, without knowing how to do anything more than drag and drop dimensions and measures onto a crosstab.

Normal pivot tables are built to create reports on non-relational data. They are very good at this. They are flexible, fast, and reasonably intuitive — once you get used to them. They start to show their limitations very quickly, however, when it comes to handling relational data that has been flattened into a single table.

For example, say we tried to run a pivot over the SQL export from our small library database. The SQL would produce a file that looks exactly the same as the original file format we tried to use for data entry.

Author	Title
Joe Bloggs	Why Libraries are great
Jane Smith	Why Libraries are great
Sam Stone	Life of Turtles
Wendy Lane	Libraries of the 22nd century
Joe Bloggs	Libraries of the 22nd century

This file format is useless for data entry, but useful for data reporting. But it is not very useful when it comes to normal pivot tables. If we wanted to count the number of unique Titles from this table, there is no simple way of doing it. You could do something dodgy, like create a new column, and use the COUNTIF formula to return a value that you can then use to calculate the number of unique titles, such as the below:

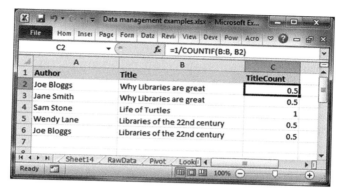

This is fine, albeit clumsy, if you want to calculate the total number of unique titles. However, what if you wanted to count how many titles Jane Smith had written? She would get the nonsense number of 0.5. You could of course adjust for this by making a combined key of author and title, and running a COUNTIF on that key. However, if you take this dodgy approach you will soon find that you need an outrageous number of columns to cater for all the reports you require. Furthermore, none of your dodgy formulas will have scope over the other dodgy formulas. So this road is way too dodgy to drive down.

PowerPivot

The better solution is PowerPivot. It is a free add on for Excel — and it has enormous functionality. I continue to be surprised by the number of professional staff who are unaware of the existence of PowerPivot — professionals that would benefit immensely from using it. PowerPivot has been built specifically for the purpose of reporting on denormalized relational data. In other words, it has been designed to report on data such as the above example, where relational data has been flattened into a single table. PowerPivot can also be used to build relationships between data, and this is something I have discussed further in the next chapter.

If we were to build a PowerPivot on our Author & Title dataset, all we would need to do is add a measure, say called DistinctTitles, and the formula would be =DISTINCTCOUNT([title]). That's it, nothing else required. And if we filtered our author to Jane Smith, we would see one distinct title. In other words, PowerPivot dynamically calculates values based on your current data view and filters used.

The second fantastic feature of PowerPivot, is that it has a suite of formulas that are designed to iterate over every row of data. The closest thing in normal Excel are array formulas, but that is about as close as a Porsche 911 is to a Trabant.

The iterating PowerPivot formulas don't just look at the current row, they loop over the entire table for each and every row. This gives you the power to write formulas that can check through all the existing data, then do something with the current row based on what you found in all the other rows. This is one of those things, where chances are you will have no idea of its potential use value until you actually are faced with a problem where you need to use such functionality. If you are working with denormalized relational data, then you will very quickly find you need formulas that can iterate over an entire table.

I will attempt to explain this with an example. Say we returned to our small library database, and we wanted to do something simple like calculate the average number of authors per title.

Author	Title
Joe Bloggs	Why Libraries are great
Jane Smith	Why Libraries are great
Sam Stone	Life of Turtles
Wendy Lane	Libraries of the 22nd century
Joe Bloggs	Libraries of the 22nd century

Because our data has been denormalized, you will find this difficult using normal Excel, and even if you did come up with something, it would be static and would not produce sensible data when you slice and dice your data. The best way to understand how row iteration works is to imagine you are manually calculating the average number of titles per author. If you were to do this manually, you would start at the first row, then scan down the list of remaining titles to count the number of titles that are the same as the current row you are in. So, for "Why Libraries are great" we find two rows, and therefore two authors. For the "Life of Turtles" we find one author, and for the "Libraries of the 22nd century" we find two authors. So that is two authors, one author and two authors, giving a total number of five authors contributing to three titles. So the average number of authors per title is 1.67. If you followed the logic carefully, you will see that to arrive at this total, we had to loop through the entire table for each row of data in the table. PowerPivot formulas can do this, where normal Excel formulas cannot. The PowerPivot measure that you could use to do the above is:

```
= AVERAGEX(
  DISTINCT(LibraryTable[title]),
    CALCULATE(COUNTROWS(LibraryTable), ALLEXCEPT(LibraryTable,
    LibraryTable[Title])
      )
  )
```

This is going to mean nothing to you right now. But I challenge you to enter the simple library database table, and after you have finished reading the next chapter, see if you can write a measure that calculates the average authors per title. Even if you don't get it right, I suspect that you will come very close to understanding the principle behind it, and if you come back to this formula after trying to do it yourself, the act of trying to solve it yourself will help you to learn. You might even find a much simpler and therefore better way of writing this formula.

How to use PowerPivot

You can download PowerPivot for free from the Microsoft website. The current (June 2015) URL is:

https://support.office.com/en-gb/article/Power-Pivot-Add-in-a9c2c6e2-cc49-4976-a7d7-40896795d045

PLEASE be aware that Microsoft can change their website at any time, so this URL might not work by the time you read this book.

Chances are you will not have administrator rights to your computer, so you will have to get your IT department to install PowerPivot. If they did install PowerPivot correctly, then the first time you start Excel you will see a message indicating that the PowerPivot add-in is loading. When you open Excel you will see a new menu ribbon for PowerPivot.

When you click on this menu you will see a few foreign options. The PowerPivot window will be the most unfamiliar thing. To access this window, click on the green PowerPivot icon on the far left of the ribbon. You have not linked PowerPivot yet to any data source, so you will just see a gray blank PowerPivot screen in the PowerPivot window.

You can link PowerPivot to many sources. For example, you can link it to text files, to Excel tables, to database tables, to database queries, and to data feeds. To link to any of these sources usually only takes a couple of clicks, and is very simple. Once data has been linked to the PowerPivot model there are four main things you can do:

- add calculated columns to the linked table
- join linked tables
- create pivot tables
- create measures for the pivot table

I will use a very simplistic Author and Title data to show how you can create a PowerPivot. The simplest way to link data in an Excel spreadsheet is to convert your data into a table, then create a "Linked Table."

To convert your data to a table, click on the Insert menu, select the data you wish to convert to a table, then click on the "Table" icon. Once you have converted a range to a table, it will look like the following:

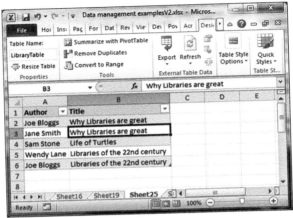

It is very good practice to name your tables something sensible, and to do this before you attempt to link PowerPivot to your table. PowerPivot can be a bit like a temperamental high end sports car at times — a very high performer, but prone to failure if not handled carefully! Notice I have named this table "LibraryTable" (see top left of above image).

Once you have converted your range to a table, and you are confident that you will not need to change the table name, the next step is to link the table to the PowerPivot model. To do this, just click on the PowerPivot ribbon, click on your table, then click on the icon "Create Linked Table." As soon as you do this the PowerPivot window will open, and you will see your table.

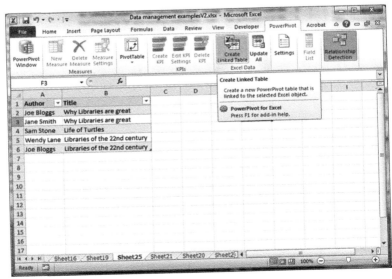

Adding calculated columns

In the PowerPivot window you will see next to your data a blank column, with the header "Add Column." To add a column you can double click on the "Add Column" header to change its title, then in any of the cells below, enter a formula.

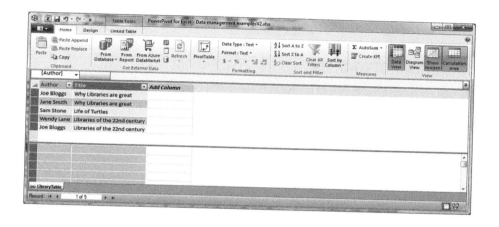

The formulas that you use in PowerPivot are very different to the ones you use in normal Excel. Where there are similarities, these can be deceptive, as the similarities can confuse you when you encounter something that does not work as you would expect. So the very first step to using PowerPivot is an emotional one, you need to accept that it is different, stop looking for the similarities with normal Excel, and expect that it will take you a little bit of time to learn.

One of the first, and perhaps most fundamental difference, is when it comes to entering formulas. In normal Excel your formulas will refer to anything from tables, to ranges, to individual cells. PowerPivot formulas share more in common with SQL than normal Excel, and they only refer to tables and columns. There is no cell A1, and you cannot type=A1+B3. The more proficient you are at normal Excel, the more time it is going to take you to adjust to this!

Creating a PowerPivot PivotTable

That's a bit of a mouthful! You can create a PivotTable either via the PowerPivot window, on the Home menu in the center of the ribbon — or alternatively you can create a pivot via the main Excel screen. To insert a pivot via the main Excel screen, click on the PowerPivot menu, then click on insert PivotTable. After you have inserted a PivotTable, you will see an empty pivot, and a field list, much like a regular PivotTable.

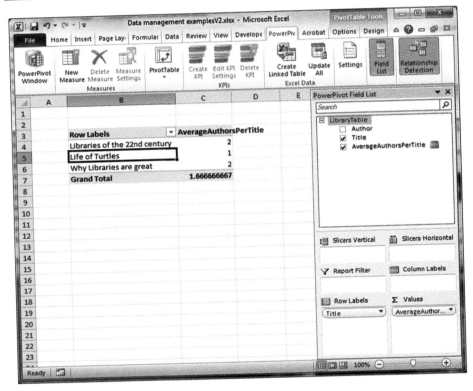

The top window includes all the tables and their fields and measures. You have only linked one table to the PowerPivot model, the "LibraryTable." Obviously, if you have not linked a table to PowerPivot, then it will not appear in the model. The measures, which will be discussed below have a calculator icon next to them. In this example, AverageAuthorsPerTitle is a measure. You will not see this measure, as you have not added it yet. Just like normal pivots, you can drag and drop fields into the Slicers, Report Filters, Column Labels, Row Labels, or Values boxes. Measures are more restrictive, and you cannot put measures anywhere except in the Values box. Depending upon how you set up your PivotTable options, you may also drag and drop directly onto the PivotTable. The Slicers function in PowerPivot is much easier to manage compared to normal Excel.

The difference between a measure and a calculated column

There will be some occasions where you could add a calculated column to the values section of the PivotTable, which raises the question, why have measures?

The answer is a calculated column is static, whereas a measure can be dynamic. Sometimes it is OK for data to be static, sometimes it is not. For example, if you wanted to count the number of books an author published in specific period, and you want to be able to change that period, from say months to years to decades, at will, then you will probably need a measure. A measure can calculate a value based on the current filters you have applied to the data, and the currently active row and column fields. A calculated column, however, is not nearly as flexible. Say, for example, taking the simple library database we used earlier, we wanted to count the number of titles produced by each author. You could include a calculated column that counts the number of times an author appeared in our table, and a calculated column to create a publication frequency distribution. But what happens, if for example, you wanted to slice and dice the data, and only look at publications within a certain period, or by the subject matter of the book (obviously our simple table had to just grow in our imagination to accommodate this example). Sure, you could filter the data down to the dataset you want to see. However, if you do this you will only see rubbish data. This is because when we include a calculated column the value it returns does not change for that row – as it does not take into account any filters that the users may have applied. If Joe Bloggs has authored two books, then the calculated column will return a value of two for each row of data relating to Joe. So, whenever we use this calculated column as a row label, and we counted the number of distinct (unique) authors in each frequency, then Joe will either be added to the frequency of two titles, or he will be excluded altogether, because we had filtered him out from the PivotTable. But what if he produced one book in 2013, and another in 2014, and we wanted to count the number of books Joe published in 2014. There is no way to get the value of one from the existing data. We could add another calculated column that counted frequency of publication by year. However, this calculated column would also be static, which means if we wanted to slice and dice the data by another field we would run into similar problems. So, measures are dynamic, calculated columns are static.

Now you might be asking, why bother with calculated columns then? Why not just use measures? The answer is that you can only uses measures as measures, i.e., as values. If you don't believe me, try dragging a measure into a row or column on a PivotTable.

Adding a measures

There are a couple of ways to add a measure. You can do it via the PowerPivot ribbon on the main Excel screen, where there is an icon called "New Measure." Alternatively, you can right click over the relevant table in the PowerPivot Field

List, and select "Add New Measure." When you do this, the Measure Settings dialogue box as shown in the next figure will open:

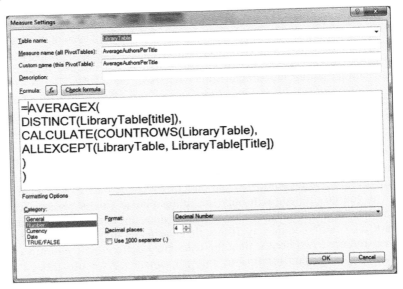

I would like to share a couple of tips that I found useful. You can zoom in on the formula by clicking on the formula window, and using the middle mouse wheel. This is very helpful for people like me with a few decades of screen fatigue under our belts. While you are in the formula window, also try adding a new line. You can do this by pressing the "Alt" plus "Enter" keys simultaneously. The formula bar shows the formula syntax, and shows a list fields as you start typing. Remember that you can set your number format in this dialogue box too.

Rather than outline generic formulas, I will take you through to the next chapter, which will demonstrate how to create a desktop library cube using PowerPivot.

How to create your own desktop library cube*

9

If you have picked up this book, and flicked straight to this chapter, you might be in for a disappointment — but hopefully not for too long. Institutionally supported multidimensional data warehouses might be sexy, and they are cutting edge for the library sector at present. However, for the most part they will be out of reach, and irrelevant, at least in the form you might have first expected and hoped for. All of the data management techniques I have discussed up to Chapter 7 might not be sexy, but they are where the real benefit lies, PROVIDED you are disciplined, and are using the data for the purpose of being good. If you have jumped straight to this chapter, it might be that you are more focused on looking good. This is fine, but if that is your main driving force behind collecting more data, then you might well end up at a point where upon completing the exercise a lot of people look at your data, including yourself, and say, OK, so what? So you will need to brace yourself for this possibility if you are primarily motivated by the search for bling.

Multidimensional data warehouses that are managed by your institution are very expensive to create and maintain. They require at least one unit that will create and manage the various data sources, and draw this into a system that staff can use to interrogate data. A cube that is created within such a system invariably requires ongoing support, in the form of training, system updates, and design changes whenever the structure of the source data changes. Furthermore, because they are such an expensive investment, the organizations that have such systems tend to have a lot of units competing to have their pet project completed. To be able to compete in this environment you need to have a very compelling story behind why the organization should dedicate expensive resources to your project, or exceptional internal political connections.

The very first thing you should be asking yourself, therefore, is why do I need an institutionally supported multidimensional data warehouse, what practical and positive change depends upon having this information, and how is this going to benefit the larger organization.

Before thinking about those questions, however, there are two things that I need to discuss. Firstly, if you had your heart set on a multidimensional data warehouse, and it now looks like I have burst your bubble in the space of a couple of paragraphs, don't lose heart, I can show you how to create what I term a "poor man's cube" using PowerPivot. To get this happening you will need two things, access to an Excel expert, and access to the relevant datasets. Once you get your head out of the "blingsphere," and into the practical world, you might actually find your "poor man's cube" can deliver real value for your library, and that you can do this really

---

Please go to the Companion Website at http://booksite.elsevier.com/9780081006634/ to download library cube materials mentioned in this chapter

fast. If you work through the PowerPivot examples, and you have a smart person who is good with Excel with a spare 10 days to work on this, there is no reason why you should not be able to get your "poor man's cube" running in 2 weeks, and absolutely purring in 2 months. The key difference, which I will discuss shortly, is that your poor man's cube will have to be based on sample data, and it will involve some manual work. The amount of manual work is still much less than would be required to run a survey, and it will be much less costly than the ongoing maintenance of an institutionally supported multidimensional data warehouse.

The second issue I need to discuss before I go any further might well be the most pressing one for you, "what is a multidimensional data warehouse, and why should I care?"

In the previous chapter I discussed relational data. I used the example of the book, in which each book might have many authors, and each author might have written many books. This is called a many-to-many relationship. I discussed how this data needs to be managed in a relational database, as it is too difficult, clumsy and unsustainable to put this information into a single flat file. Remember a flat file is a single table, with column headers under which data is placed in rows.

Well, when it comes to books, for example, the many-to-many relationships extend well beyond the bibliographic details of a given publication. The author of a book, for example, might have many institutional and research group affiliations, they might have received many grants, they might teach many students, and each of those students might study several subjects, and the list goes on and on. The world of a relational database is typically a very small one, and it is usually focused around a small set of processes. For example, the database used to hold student data usually only contains the data needed to manage and confer a qualification. Databases for staff usually only contain just the information needed to manage their employment. Library management systems usually only contain enough information to help facilitate the discovery and lending of material.

What a multidimensional data warehouse does is take a small number of relational databases, and join them together. The databases are joined together for the sole purpose of getting new data out. Because these data warehouses are not used for data entry, but only data reporting, they do not have to use the same data structure as relational databases. Relational databases use what is called a normalized table structure, and the purpose of this is to ensure data integrity during data entry. Because these data warehouses are only fetching data, they are designed in manner that optimizes data reporting. There are relationships created in these warehouses, but they tend to follow what is called a star scheme, with the Fact Table in the middle, and the tables containing the dimensions individually linked to the Fact Table. So the relationships in these systems tend to be very simple compared to their relational database cousins.

The Fact Table contains the lowest level of data you want the system to be able to report on. Data can always be rolled up to a higher level (with the right rules in place!), but you cannot drill down below the smallest grain of data you have collected. For example, if you had a tally of the total number of visits during the day (i.e., just a single number for the day), and someone asked you how many people visited between 10 and 11 am, then you would not be able to answer that question. The same logic applies to the Fact Table, it can only report on the information contained in the table.

This is a very simplistic and short overview of multidimensional data warehouses, and I am by no means an expert. However, just as you don't need to know how a car engine works to be able to drive a car effectively, you don't need a software engineering degree to understand the benefits of a multidimensional data warehouse.

If you work in an academic library, you will have records stored in some format covering who is using your resources. Your institution will have information on students, including demographic and academic data. Your institution will also have systems that store information about academic staff, perhaps even their publication history. The benefit of a multidimensional data warehouse is that it allows you to answer questions that otherwise cannot be answered if the student, staff, and library data are kept in separate silos. For example, it would be impossible to identify with any degree of certainty whether your most successful researchers are making higher use of your collection than less successful researchers. By joining these individual databases together, you can answer that question.

I do not know the etymology of the term cube as it applies to multidimensional data warehouses, but whatever its origin, it is an apt description. Cast your mind back to the 1980s, when rubrix cubes were all the rage. The warehouses are much like the rubrix cube, where each face of the cube is a different database. Just like the rubrix cube allows you to slide one face over another, so too the warehouse allows you to slide one database over another. If one face of the cube is staff data, another student data, and another library data — then the cube allows you to slide one over the other, so you can do things like look at student usage of library resources by their demographic profile.

If you are a public library, then there are fewer opportunities for joining datasets to find answers to important questions. Your council might hold some data on rate payers, but even in the unlikely event that you could get your hands on such data, it is unlikely to be in a format that will allow you to join the datasets up. Don't despair, this chapter is at the bling end of town, and there are probably a lot of things that you can do to improve your day-to-day data management, on which all the preceding chapters have been focused. Notwithstanding this, it is worth understanding how more sophisticated data can be created from joining discrete data sources, as you never know what opportunities might arise.

To join up a number of different databases you need to be able to do two things. First and foremost you need something to join the data on, and it has to be robust. Things like names are no good. Many people might have the name Joe Smith, or there might even be many people with the name Brian Cox. The thing you are joining the datasets on needs to be unique, and it has to be something that does not change. Joining student data with library usage data was possible at the University of Wollongong because the students have a unique identifier, and that same identifier is used in all data locations. Well, strictly speaking that is not correct, as the ezproxy logs contained student usernames, whereas the library management system contained student numbers. However, each student had one student number, and one username, and both those things are unique to that student, and neither change over time. So this means everything could still be joined up, it just needed an additional table to link student numbers with their student usernames. Finding a unique identifier is not an easy task, and if you can't get past that stage, then you can't go any further.

The next step is always achievable, though it requires patience, consultation, and liberal amounts of intelligence. You cannot just join up unique identifiers from two different databases and walk away expecting the computer to go off and do all the magic. A squashed ant has more intelligence than a computer. For the computer to do the magic, you have to tell it what to do — and you have to tell it for each and every step. This is where the hard graft comes in, and if you are fortunate enough for your institution to be able to build a cube for you, then the data warehouse experts will have to spend a lot of time with you developing what they will call "business rules" for determining how to join the data — and they will have to spend even longer writing these rules up in a manner that a computer will understand. For example, if a student borrowed a book outside of session, and you want to be able to join up borrowing with student marks, then you will need a rule in place to deal with these circumstances. If a student has borrowed a book, and you want to be able to see student borrowing by their faculty, then you are going to need rules in place to deal with situations where a student is enrolled in more than one faculty. You can imagine that these rules can become quite complex.

At the University of Wollongong we created a cube joining library usage data from the Library Management System and the ezproxy logs to student demographic and grades data. The business rules for this cube were relatively simple, compared to say a student attrition cube. If you do have access to an institutionally supported data warehouse, then creating your own library cube might be a viable option. The technical hurdles are not that significant, and you will need to sort these out in the context of the specific peculiarities of your institution's data. The biggest hurdles are the political issues. Very briefly, if you do want to go down the road of creating an institutionally supported library cube, some the key things you will need to do include:

- Investigate whether there are any show stoppers. Do you have the data, does it have the required identifiers, is the data accessible? The biggest potential showstopper is privacy. If you don't have a privacy consent that will cover use of the data for the cube, then it is most likely game over for this particular project. Get a copy of the privacy consent, study it well and form your own opinion on its scope, then seek the opinion of your legal unit. Make sure you understand the issues before you seek advice from your legal unit. They are very busy, and if they think your request is not important, there is a chance they might just say no to avoid having to dedicate time to the request.
- Identify an absolute rock solid business case, and one that is not just about your library. You will be asking your institution to embark on a project that will require the involvement of many IT specialists, in scoping, requirements, building, testing, maintenance, and training. You would not do any of this without a very compelling business case, so don't expect anything less from your institution.
- Make sure the director of the IT staff that will need to create the cube is on board. Communicate your vision to them in a compelling and concise way, see how they respond, and be prepared to have to sell your idea. If you think they are on board, then find out realistically how this project might fit in with their priorities.

- Make a formal business case — in whatever way that is expected to be made at your organization.
- Identify the business rules. I identified some very simple logic that was then used to build many of the business rules. The basic premise is that you cannot go backward in time. If a student had borrowed an item, then whatever academic benefit they might have received from reading it cannot be applied to subjects they completed before they borrowed that item. The other basic premise was that I wanted to avoid double counting. This had two major consequences. The grain of the data had to be quite coarse, which is actually a pun! If a student borrowed a book, then I had no way of knowing which subject they used it for. Given that almost all students are studying many subjects, this meant I could not include subject level data in the cube. I had to have faculty level data in the cube, however, and I decided to deal with this by splitting usage across the faculties on a pro-rata basis. So if a student borrowed one item, and studied within two faculties, the borrowing was split between the faculties. This is arbitrary, and theoretically could introduce a lot of noise into the data. However, in practice most students are studying in one faculty; plus I found very little difference in results when comparing the data for those who were studying in one faculty, compared to those studying at more than one. The second consequence of these two simple business rules was that one cube could not be built that would meet all my requirements. I wanted to be able to match student performance data to library usage, in order to be able to showcase the library. However, this data only makes the library look good, it does not help it to be good. So more than anything else I wanted data on how resources were being used on a weekly basis by student demographic, so as that I could accurately assess the impact of the library's promotional activities. This required that the forward allocation of resource usage that occurred out of session for the value cube, had to be brought backward to the week level for the marketing cube. So the logic behind the date dimensions was so different it required two cubes. It is best that you develop your own business rules independently, because this is the only way you will develop a good understanding of the data structure, and this understanding is needed to be able to use the cube properly.
- Be available at short notice, and be prepared for the long haul. If your institution does support your project, there is a good chance that other projects will knock yours to the back of the queue from time-to-time. If the IT staff have a short window of opportunity to take on fresh work, you want to ensure that they will come to you. So stay in contact, know what progress is being made, understand their own priorities, and know when they can fit in your project. Be flexible, knowledgeable, approachable, reasonable, positive, but firm. Also, recognize achievement, progress and provide authentic recognition. They might not report to the library, but they are nevertheless providing a service to the library. So treat them as you would like to be treated.

Chances are you will not be able to build an institutionally supported library cube. However, this does not mean you cannot do the next best thing. You can collect a sample of data that will be more compelling, accurate, detailed and insightful than anything you could do with a survey.

Personally I think most surveys are a waste of time. For the most part they are asking respondents to give opinions on things that they most likely never considered before, until the survey was pushed under their nose. So what do they do? They respond with what they think they should say. If a library is working very well, then clients might breeze through the place without noticing the library's efforts. This does not mean the library did not do a good job. A poorly laid out library might rely very heavily on signage, an information desk or automated kiosk, and perhaps even roving staff. But if a client was highly satisfied by the helpful staff that told them where to find a resource in one library, and another did not have to ask anyone to find it in the other — then what result is the survey likely to provide for both libraries? That the first was helpful, and the second was not?

I am not saying there is no place for qualitative data. But to do it properly, i.e., to get valid and reliable data that tells you something more than you already know, and something you can act on, is a very costly and involved exercise. If on the other hand, you wanted some basic information to determine whether a promotion was successful, or you wanted to see whether usage of a particular resource improved after an information literacy class, or you wanted to show how the library was contributing to improved academic performance, then interrogating a sample of your system logs will provide better data than you could get from any survey.

If building a cube for a multidimensional data warehouse is a huge undertaking, then in comparison you could build a "poor man's" cube in a short space of time, either by yourself, or using an Excel expert.

However, just because a cube might now be in your reach does not mean you should take shortcuts. First and foremost you MUST sort out the privacy issues. If your students have not given consent for this sort of use, then it will be game over. You cannot put your institution's reputation at risk by behaving like a cowboy. Go over the student privacy consent form thoroughly, and identify at what point in the student lifecycle they signed the form. If you believe that your project is covered by the consent, seek advice from your legal unit. Obviously, if you are not the Library Director, you will need to talk to them before you do anything. If you can use the data, your obligations do not stop there. You should discuss with your legal unit what you need to do to ensure the privacy of the information is not compromised by your project. For example, you should save any files containing personal information, such as ezproxy logs, to a location that only authorized staff will be able to access. This data has value, and the correct usage of it will deliver value to students, you just need to be aware of your privacy obligations, and ensure they are followed.

Making the "desktop cube"

I may have been a bit generous with the title "desk top cube," or even "poor man's cube," as we will simply be combining a couple of flat files. However, despite the simplicity of this "cube" you will make, there is still quite a lot you will be able to do with it.

There are a few things that you will need to do to create this cube. Getting the datasets will take the longest, because chances are you will be relying on other people to make this happen. However, the rest of the work should only take a couple of days, or 2 weeks if you are dealing with unanticipated and complex problems. The caveat is that you are getting someone smart and motivated to work on this task, and someone that is reasonably good at learning new things and comfortable working with Excel. So, if you can tick this box, the job of creating your own desktop cube will involve:

* Sourcing the datasets
* Merging the datasets
* Linking PowerPivot to the merged dataset
* Creating additional tables within PowerPivot
* Writing calculated columns
* Creating relationships
* Writing measures
* Using the data as intended

This is one of those projects where all the steps need to be completed sequentially. If you skip any of these steps, then your cube will not work. So, please be patient, and follow this step-by-step.

Sourcing the datasets

The first step is to get access to a couple of data sets. You will need a log that contains information about student usage of library resources. If your students are able to access resources without authenticating, then you might be in for some problems. Talk to the IT staff in your library about how to get access to the logs. The logs are enormous, so you will most likely have to limit your data to a sample of logs. Check with your university statistician about what sample size you need to collect in order to be able to make inferences about your student population. You will need to consider how much chance you are willing to take that your sample does not reflect the characteristics of the general population within what you deem to be an acceptable degree of error, but this is something you can discuss with your statistician. Here is a screenshot of some of the ezproxy log file I have used for this demonstration cube. This is not real data.

The logs will need to contain at the very least two things, a unique student identifier, and something useful to group the data, such as a time-date stamp.

You will need at least one more dataset, a flat file containing information about students, including a unique identifier that you can use to link to information from your student file to the log file. If one system uses "usernames," and another uses "student numbers," then you will have to get a table that includes the usernames for every student number. You can then use this table as an intermediary — to join the two data sets up.

Your student data file might contain things such as gender and age. The thing to keep in mind, is that some of the data you ask for might result in several rows of data for each student. For example, students will have only one gender, but if you ask for information on their faculty, then you may end up with multiple rows of data for some students. This is because some students may only be enrolled in one faculty, but others may be enrolled in several. Now, an institutionally supported data warehouse can deal with this easily. However, we are making a pragmatic desktop version, and even though PowerPivot is fantastic, it cannot work miracles.

I have set up PowerPivot in this example so as all the student data is imported in the LibraryUsage table (or the "Fact Table" to be more precise). I have done this to avoid the escalating complexity that occurs when you try to use PowerPivot to manage many-to-many relationships via its internal model. One student may have many rows of data in the ezproxy log, and if they have more than one row of data in the student table, then viola, you have many-to-many relationships. I will show you how to create a single flat file that contains almost all the data you need to set up your own desktop library cube. However, the cost of this simplicity is that the data structure is not optimal. I will explain this with an example. If you have a student that belongs to two faculties, and they have 1000 rows of data in the ezproxy log, then the structured query language (SQL) I am about to show you will create 2000 rows of data for the LibraryUsage table. If you had ten rows of data for a given student, and that student had 3000 rows of data against their name in the ezproxy log, then that student alone would have 30,000 rows of data. As you can imagine, given that the ezproxy logs you are working with might easily contain half a million records just for one day, the number of rows of data generated by trying to join up many-to-many records would soon become too enormous for even PowerPivot. So my advice is this, try to ask for data that will not generate more than one row per student, or only on rare occasions more than one row. This is easy enough if you are creative. For example, if you are interested in the geographic location of your clients, then don't ask for student data by every address they have ever resided at, only ask for their most recent address. That way you will only get one row of data for each student.

Where do you get the student data? Every institution is different, so you will need to do a bit of detective work. Universities often have a dedicated data unit, so find out where that is, and start talking with them. Make sure you have a clear idea of what you want, and how you want that data structured before you go and see them.

Here is a screenshot of some of the student data I used for the demonstration cube. Once again, the data is not real.

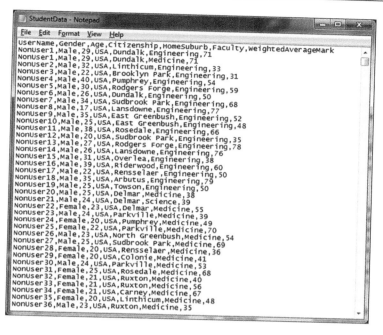

```
StudentData - Notepad
File  Edit  Format  View  Help
UserName,Gender,Age,Citizenship,HomeSuburb,Faculty,WeightedAverageMark
NonUser1,Male,29,USA,Dundalk,Engineering,71
NonUser1,Male,29,USA,Dundalk,Medicine,71
NonUser2,Male,32,USA,Linthicum,Engineering,33
NonUser3,Male,22,USA,Brooklyn Park,Engineering,31
NonUser4,Male,40,USA,Pumphrey,Engineering,54
NonUser5,Male,30,USA,Rodgers Forge,Engineering,59
NonUser6,Male,26,USA,Dundalk,Engineering,50
NonUser7,Male,34,USA,Sudbrook Park,Engineering,68
NonUser8,Male,17,USA,Lansdowne,Engineering,77
NonUser9,Male,35,USA,East Greenbush,Engineering,52
NonUser10,Male,25,USA,East Greenbush,Engineering,48
NonUser11,Male,38,USA,Rosedale,Engineering,66
NonUser12,Male,20,USA,Sudbrook Park,Engineering,35
NonUser13,Male,27,USA,Rodgers Forge,Engineering,78
NonUser14,Male,26,USA,Lansdowne,Engineering,76
NonUser15,Male,31,USA,Overlea,Engineering,38
NonUser16,Male,39,USA,Riderwood,Engineering,60
NonUser17,Male,22,USA,Rensselaer,Engineering,50
NonUser18,Male,35,USA,Arbutus,Engineering,79
NonUser19,Male,25,USA,Towson,Engineering,50
NonUser20,Male,25,USA,Delmar,Medicine,38
NonUser21,Male,24,USA,Delmar,Science,39
NonUser22,Female,23,USA,Delmar,Medicine,55
NonUser23,Male,24,USA,Parkville,Medicine,39
NonUser24,Female,20,USA,Pumphrey,Medicine,49
NonUser25,Female,22,USA,Parkville,Medicine,70
NonUser26,Male,23,USA,North Greenbush,Medicine,54
NonUser27,Male,25,USA,Sudbrook Park,Medicine,69
NonUser28,Female,20,USA,Rensselaer,Medicine,36
NonUser29,Female,20,USA,Colonie,Medicine,41
NonUser30,Male,24,USA,Parkville,Medicine,53
NonUser31,Female,25,USA,Rosedale,Medicine,68
NonUser32,Female,21,USA,Ruxton,Medicine,40
NonUser33,Female,21,USA,Ruxton,Medicine,56
NonUser34,Female,21,USA,Carney,Medicine,67
NonUser35,Female,20,USA,Linthicum,Medicine,48
NonUser36,Male,23,USA,Ruxton,Medicine,35
```

Using MS Access to create a merged dataset

Once you have these two data sets, the next step is to join them up. I have used MS Access to import the files (as linked tables so they are easy to update), and I also used MS Access to join the tables. I then point my PowerPivot to the query I have written in MS Access. This set up is the simplest one I could think of, and one that makes it easy to import new data into your library cube.

In this example I refer to the "ezproxy log." Your institution may use a different log, and a different system. However, the principles are the same. Whatever the log file is called, if your institution has one, it should contain a unique user identifier, and additional data, such as the time and date, and the URL being activated.

Unfortunately the ezproxy log I am using has multiple delimiters, which means there are a couple of hoops you need to jump through to import the data into a system where you can join it with your student data. You could clean it up a bit with a Schema.ini file, or use SQL to clean it up. If you know how to do this, then go ahead and do that. If this is all babble to you, then use MS Access, the wizards will make things easy. The headers I want to keep are "UserName," "IP address," "Date," and "URL string." I created a linked file, that way I can easily overwrite the file with new logs, and then simply hit refresh in PowerPivot to bring in the new data.

To create a linked table in MS Access, click on import a text file. In MS Access 2010, this is on the "External Data" tab.

Once you have done this, a wizard box will open. Click Browse to point to your source data, then click on "Link to the data source by creating a linked table," as shown below.

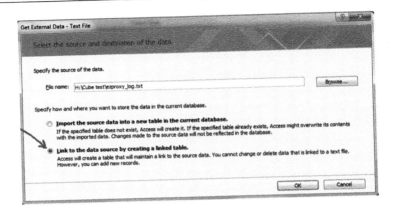

After you click OK, a new dialogue will open. Select delimited, choose space delimiter, then click on the advanced tab in the bottom left of the link Text Wizard, and set the options to reflect your file structure as shown in the below screenshot. As there are no column headers in my data, you need to change the column headers from the defaults (e.g., "Field1"), which are not very intuitive. Failure to change these will make your formulas indecipherable later on. I changed the UrlString field to a memo data type, as this is the largest text data type in MS Access, and some of these strings are very large. You have also noticed that I have chosen to skip some fields, rather than import nonsense data. The nonsense data is a product of my log file using multiple delimiters. Your log file may not have this problem.

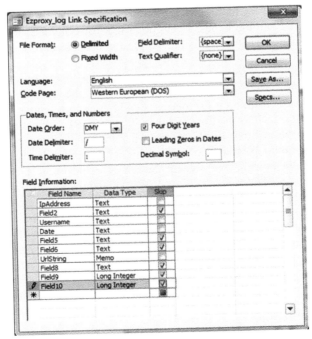

Once you have done this, click OK.

To import the student data into your Access database, simply repeat the above process. Your student data will probably come to you as a CSV file, but if it comes as an Excel file, it's easy enough just to do a save as "*.csv" file.

Once you have both the student and log data in Access, the next step is to create a query that will join the two tables, and spit out a single table containing all the data you need for your PowerPivot model. To do this in Access 2010, open the "Create" menu, and click on "Query Design." This will then open up the "Show Table" dialogue box. You need to add both tables, i.e., the ezproxy_log and the StudentData tables. Next, you need to create a join between the two tables, and you do this by dragging your username from one table, onto the username in the other table. You will be able to choose between three types of joins, and you MUST pick the right one. The correct join is where you will include all records from "StudentData," and only those records from "Ezproxy_log" where the joined fields are equal (see below).

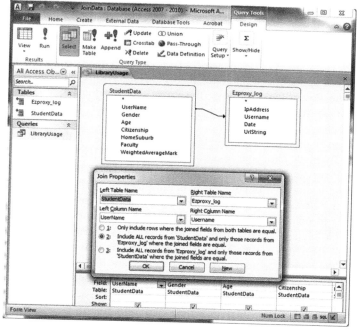

This join will ensure that even if a student did not use a library resource, they will be included in the query. The inclusion of nonusers allows you to run queries in PowerPivot to answer questions such as "what proportion of the student cohort are using library resources?" Finally, you need to select what you wish to see in the report. You could double click on the * at the top of both tables, and this would add everything from both tables. The problem with doing this is that you will have two fields for username, and both will contain exactly the same info. So, for the sake of spending a few minutes more now, it's worth the saving on confusion you will have at the PowerPivot end. So it is better to add all the fields you need manually. You can manually add a field by double clicking on it. You should then save your query. I saved it as "LibraryUsage." This name will then become the name of our "Fact Table" in our PowerPivot model.

You have now done everything you need to do in Access, so you can close it down. Make sure all your files are securely saved to the same location. By all your files I mean the student raw data, the ezproxy log file, the Access files, and the Excel file containing the PowerPivot, i.e., everything. If you scatter these files everywhere, it will just make managing the files more difficult and increase your risk of an accidental privacy breach.

I have explained how to merge data using Access, as many people are familiar with it, and if you are not, chances are you will be able to find someone that is. It is possible, however, to do the merge entirely within Excel, using something like the Microsoft Power Query for Excel, which like PowerPivot is also a free add on. I avoided this, because in this instance I think it just makes the learning curve too steep given the task at hand is to create a usable desktop cube within a short space of time.

Linking PowerPivot to the merged dataset

Open up a fresh spreadsheet, and save it to the same secure location as your other files. Open the PowerPivot window (the green icon on the far left). If you don't know how to do this, go back to the PowerPivot chapter; you really should read that chapter before this one anyway.

As I previously discussed, you can hook into a multitude of different sources using PowerPivot. To hook into your Access Query, click on the "Home" menu on the green PowerPivot Screen, then click on the "From Database" icon. One of your options will be to import from Access. Click on it. The "Table Import Wizard" will open. Click on "Browse," and open your Access database, and click next. The simplest option is to point directly to your query, and you can do this by checking the radio button for "Select" from a list of tables and views to choose the data to import. Click "Next," then make sure you have checked the box next to LibraryUsage (or whatever the name was that you created earlier for the joined tables in Access). Once you have done this, the table will import. You should see something like this:

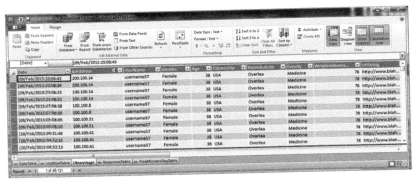

Congratulations, you are now almost half way there! Save this file as "Library Desktop Cube.xlsx," that way you will know what workbook I am referring to when I say "Library Desktop Cube"!

There are a couple of more tables you need to create. These are not absolutely necessary, but they will add more depth to the reports you can get out of your data, and help you to learn how to do a few nifty tricks using PowerPivot.

Adding a few more tables

There are four tables that we need to manually add to the spreadsheet:

- IP address table
- Resources table
- Frequency table
- Date table

IP address table

The IP Address Table will enable you to be able to determine the campus students were accessing your resources from. In this example, I have created a table called LocationTable, into which I have entered location for computers by campus.

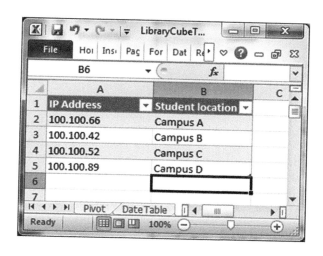

To link this table to the PowerPivot model, you need to click on the PowerPivot ribbon, and click on the "Create Linked Table" icon.

You may or may not be interested in looking at the IP address data. If not, you may still find it useful to understand the scope of what is possible.

Resources table

This table that is arguably one of the most useful, and it is also the most complex.

The purpose of the ezproxy logs is to manage the authentication process. Most subscription resources are subject to license agreements that require you to limit access to authorized users. One of the by-products of the authentication process is the ezproxy log. This log contains a URL string that is generated as part of the authentication and database access process. Within this URL string are fragments that can be used to uniquely identify the resource that is being accessed. For example, if a client is accessing Scopus, the URL string returned will include the text "scopus.com." You can then use these unique fragments to piece together a story on what clients are using, and also perhaps more interestingly, what they are not using. I have called this table "ResourceTable." To link this table to the PowerPivot model, you need to click on the PowerPivot ribbon, and click on the "Create Linked Table" icon.

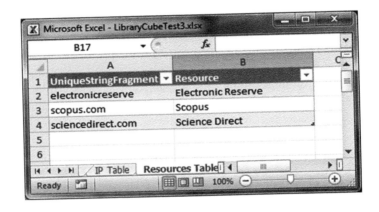

Frequency table

The purpose of the frequency table is to allow you to use the pivot table to easily group usage of library resources by predefined frequencies. Putting this data in a separate table achieves two things: it makes for much cleaner formulas; and it allows you to easily edit the frequency ranges. The ranges you select should cover all possible uses, from the minimal amount of use possible (which will always be zero), up to the maximum usage possible. The first column is the text you will see in your pivot table. The "Start" column defines the beginning of the range, and the "Stop" column the end of the range. So, for example, if Joe Bloggs was actively retrieving library resources for 20 min, then their frequency of usage would be 16 to 30. I have called this table "FreqMinutesDayTable." To link this table to the PowerPivot model, you need to click on the PowerPivot ribbon, and click on the "Create Linked Table" icon.

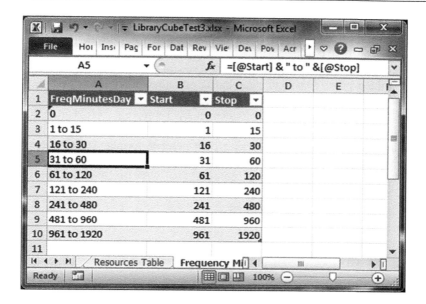

Date table

The last table to add is the date table. This is probably not so important given that you will only be using a sample of logs, and it is highly unlikely that there will be zero usage in any time period. Nevertheless, a date table might be useful for something else, like visits data, and therefore this is a good opportunity to practice the concept of using date tables. The purpose of a date table is to ensure that you can report on dates that are not used in the Fact Table. For example, say we wanted to report on the number of unique students using library resources by hour, but no one used the library between 2 am and 5 am. If you have no usage between those hours, then that data will not be in your "LibraryUsage" table. This means, when you produce a pivot table for library usage by hour, the table will not include any information for these times. This means any graphs you run off the data will have scales that jump from 1 am to 6 am. You want to be able to easily see when the library resources are not being used; you don't want to have to scan down the row labels to work out which periods are missing. Rather, you want to be able to see: 2 am − zero usage, 3 am − zero usage, etc. Creating a date table is one way of ensuring the "zero usage" periods are clearly reported. A date table also has other benefits, such as removing the clutter from your Fact Table.

To create a working date table, you need to have a row of data for each and every period you wish to report upon. In other words, you need to think of the lowest level of granularity you want to report on. The date table could be placed in another database, a csv file, etc. I have put the date table into "Library Desktop Cube.xlsx." The first step to creating a date table is to start entering the data on a new worksheet. I created a table containing a row of data for each and every minute covered in the ezproxy logs, and some buffer on either side just to show you how it works. Don't worry, you don't have to type hundreds of times, just enter the starting time, then use a formula to increment it by 1 min (e.g., =A2+(1/24/60), then paste down). Date and times can undo a few people. Make sure all the cells containing a date and time are formatted as a date number format. I prefer to go with custom formatting, and chose d/mm/yyyy h:m:ss. You need to use the same date format in your date table, as the column you wish to join against in your LibraryUsage table. Once you have a list of all the times, you can then use formulas to roll your data up into Day, Month, etc.

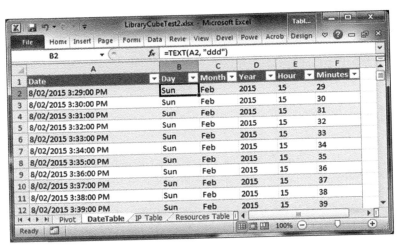

I have called this table "DateTable." To link this table to the PowerPivot model, you need to click on the PowerPivot ribbon, and click on the "Create Linked Table" icon. In this instance I have added the formulas into the table, just to show that it is possible to "mix and match" old and new Excel, however you would be better off limiting the table to column A, and using PowerPivot to calculate the fields in columns B through to F. This is because PowerPivot can crunch numbers with a lot more speed than normal Excel. It is also a tidier model to have all your calculations in PowerPivot, rather than some scattered in the source tables, and others in PowerPivot calculated columns. If you wanted to add Day, Month, etc. as calculated columns in PowerPivot, here are the formulas:

- Minute = MINUTE([Date])
- Hour = HOUR([Date])
- Day = FORMAT([Date], "DDD")
- Month = FORMAT([Date], "MMM")
- Year = YEAR([Date])

Adding calculated columns to PowerPivot

Once all the tables have been created the next step is to add formulas to the PowerPivot model. The formulas and their basic functions include:

- FormattedDate — a cleaned up version of the date
- ResourceUsed — the resource users accessed
- KeyMinutesActive — a combined key used to identify minutes of usage
- KeyYearMonthDay — a combined key used to identify minutes of usage per day
- FrequencyMinutesTotal — users frequency of usage over the whole dataset
- FrequencyMinutesDay — users frequency of usage for a day
- Location — the location users accessed library resources from
- GroupMinutesDay — a frequency distribution for minutes per day
- GroupMinutesTotal — a frequency for minutes usage calculated over the whole dataset

Remember you need to go to the PowerPivot window to be able to add these calculated columns to the "LibraryUsage" table.

FormattedDate

The ezproxy logs I had to work with did not have consistent delimiters. This meant I had two choices, write some SQL or script to clean it up, or just import the date in a dirty format, and show you how to clean it up at the PowerPivot end. I choose the later! The date contains a stray "[" character as the start of the string. It's always there, so that makes it very easy to remove. The day, month, year and time always occupy the same position, which also makes it very easy to parse the text. It is much more difficult to parse text when it is inconsistent. Luckily, that is not the case.

To create a calculated column, open the PowerPivot window, and make sure you are in the DataView. Then open the LibraryUsage table. The tables in the PowerPivot model can be access much the same way you access different sheets in normal Excel, i.e., they are accessed via tabs in the bottom left of the window. To add a new column, scroll to the left until you see a blank column with the header "Add Column." Click on that column heading to change its name, and click on any of the cells below to insert a formula. The formula you will be adding is:

    =IF(ISBLANK([IpAddress]), BLANK(), MID([Date],2, 11) &" "& MID([Date],14, 5)
    &":00")

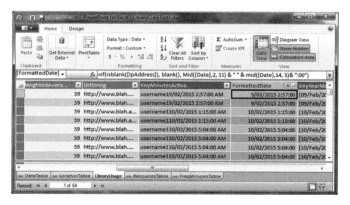

Here is how the formula works:

- =if(**ISBLANK([IpAddress])**), BLANK(), MID([Date],2, 11) &" "& MID([Date],14, 5) &":00") The bolded part of the formula checks if there is a value in the IpAddress column, and if it is blank, then it executes the "BLANK()" command. In other words, if there is no IP address, then just make the FormattedDate column blank. As you will recall, this table includes nonusers. If a student did not use a library resource, then they cannot have data for a date. Therefore we also want the FormattedDate column to be blank for nonusers.
- =if(ISBLANK([IpAddress]), BLANK(), **MID([Date],2, 11)** &" "& MID([Date],14, 5) &":00") The bolded formula pulls out the text from the date column, starting at the second character in the string, and grabbing everything for a further 11 characters. This command surgically removes the "[" character, and stops just at the end of the date.
- =if(ISBLANK([IpAddress]), BLANK(), MID([Date],2, 11) &" "& **MID([Date],14, 5) &":00"**) The last (bolded) bit of the formula also surgically removes a few characters from the date string, starting at the 14th character, and taking the next five characters. I then added the string ":00" at the end. This was to get rid of the data on seconds. The lowest grain I am interested in looking at is minutes, so by rounding the seconds off to zero, it makes the task of counting unique entries at the minute level much easier. The reason why I did this will become more apparent as you read on.

ResourceUsed

I am being mean, and starting early with the hardest formula. If you don't get this formula, press on to the other formulas, and then come back later.

There is really nothing to join the ResourceTable to the LibraryUsage table, so this where the formula has to do the hard work. Within the LibraryUsageTable I created a calculated column (called "ResourceUsed") in the LibraryUsage table into which I entered the formula:

```
=if(ISBLANK([FormattedDate]), BLANK(), if(ISBLANK(lookupvalue(ResourcesTable
[Resource],ResourcesTable[UniqueStringFragment],FIRSTNONBLANK(FILTER
(VALUES(ResourcesTable[UniqueStringFragment]),FIND(ResourcesTable
[UniqueStringFragment],LibraryUsage[UrlString],1,0)),1))), "Unknown", LOOKUPVALUE
(ResourcesTable[Resource],ResourcesTable[UniqueStringFragment],FIRSTNONBLANK
(FILTER(VALUES(ResourcesTable[UniqueStringFragment]),FIND(ResourcesTable
[UniqueStringFragment],LibraryUsage[UrlString],1,0)),1))))
```

Now, this formula is big, and it even scares me a bit!! I had to do a bit of googling to find a formula that could do what I needed, and came across this fantastic website called "PowerPivot(pro)," where I saw that Rob had blogged the answer to a similar need: http://www.powerpivotpro.com/2014/01/containsx-finding-if-a-value-in-table-1-has-a-matching-value-in-table-2/.

My formula looks twice as scary as it actually is, because it essentially contains the formula twice, once to see if the UrlString does contain a fragment, and if it does, return the resource name for that fragment, and if it does not, return the text "unknown." I am also using a nested IF statement, with the first level asking, "Is the date blank?," and if the answer is yes, then return a blank, otherwise go off and do some work on finding the fragment. So the real core to the formula is this:

```
LOOKUPVALUE(ResourcesTable[Resource],ResourcesTable[UniqueStringFragment],
FIRSTNONBLANK(FILTER(VALUES(ResourcesTable[UniqueStringFragment]),FIND
(ResourcesTable[UniqueStringFragment],LibraryUsage[UrlString],1,0)),1))
```

If you are struggling with formulas, it can help to write them with indenting, so as that you can visualize them more easily. So here is the same formula again, but this time with indents:

```
LOOKUPVALUE(ResourcesTable[Resource],ResourcesTable[UniqueStringFragment],
    FIRSTNONBLANK(
      FILTER(
        VALUES(ResourcesTable[UniqueStringFragment]),
          FIND(ResourcesTable[UniqueStringFragment], LibraryUsage[UrlString],1,0)
          )
        ,1)
      )
```

The first part of the formula is simply a lookup. The data I want to find is in the ResourcesTable[Resource] column, and the place I am searching is the ResourcesTable[UniqueStringFragment] column. So, if I find a fragment that matches a value in the ResourcesTable[UniqueStringFragment], the table will return the corresponding row in the ResourcesTable[Resource] column. For example, if I find the fragment "sciencedirect.com," the LOOKUPVALUE formula will return "Science Direct."

The FIRSTNONBLANK formula looks through every row in a column, testing to see if an expression returns anything other than a blank. As soon as FIRSTNONBLANK finds something other than a blank, it stops, and returns that value. The test, or the expression part of the formula, is looking to see if the UniqueStringFragment is located in the UrlString column in the LibraryUsage table. The VALUES and FILTER sections of the formula are designed to provide a column that the FIRSTNONBLANK formula is expecting, but narrowed down to the specific record where the fragment has been found.

The hard bit about understanding these sorts of formulas is coming to terms with how the PowerPivot formulas can iterate through every row to test an expression. This is something that is very new for Excel, and it can take people a while to adjust their thinking on how to write formulas — particularly if you are very used to normal Excel. The other thing you may struggle with is the concept of filtering. In many ways the building blocks of PowerPivot formulas, DAX, shares more in common with SQL than traditional Excel formulas. But within this difficulty, also lies the amazing abilities of PowerPivot. So, if you are struggling and you want to understand how PowerPivot formulas work, start with something very simple, and very small, and experiment. Build your understanding slowly.

So, hopefully this formula has not scared you too much, but if it has, just accept that you don't get it for the moment, and move on. You can always plug it into your Library PowerPivot, and fiddle with the parts that need to fit to your data, without having to fully understand how the formula works. Mind you, make sure you test the results, and you test them in at least three places. You might not fully understand the formula, but you will know what results you should be getting, so you will be able to test it.

Testing is always essential, but it is even more essential if you don't fully understand how a formula works. Regardless of how confident you are, you must always test to ensure that the data results match the results you would expect. There are many ways to do this. One way is to manually calculate the results you would expect to see from at least three different views of the data, then test whether the data returned in your pivots matches your manual calculations. They should always match precisely. Near enough is never good enough – as the result might be close due to the way you have set up a given view, and it might be wildly off for a different view (i.e., a different combination of calculated columns, measures, row and column labels and filters applied to your pivot). So test, test, and test some more.

KeyMinutesActive

Some formulas are added so as that you can use them directly as row or column headers in a pivot table, others are created as stepping stones to the final formula that produces something useful for the pivot table. This formula is a stepping stone. The KeyMinutesActive formula creates a combined key that is used to identify minutes of usage. Strictly speaking, the combined keys are unnecessary as they could be eliminated by using the SUMMARIZE function. However, this would have made the learning curve too steep in this instance.

In the previous chapter I discussed the difference between calculated columns and measures, explaining that measures are dynamic, but they cannot be used to aggregate data under column rows or headers. The frequency distribution in this data is a good example of these differences. In order to be able to produce a frequency distribution in a pivot table I need the data to sit in a column, not a measure. I don't have a column in the raw data that provides a frequency of usage, so I have to create a formula in a calculated column to identify the frequency of usage for each row. However, the frequency needs to cover a particular period. For example, it could be the frequency of usage for the whole data set, or it might be frequency of usage over a day. This is where things become difficult.

I will explain this with an example. If a student spent 2 min accessing a resource on 1 day, and 50 min on another, then the results I get in the frequency distribution are going to be different depending upon whether I am looking at the total minutes in the data (52 min), or the usage on the first day (2 min). If I wanted to see how much students were accessing the resources on a daily basis, then the formula needs to be constructed to identify how many minutes of access occurred for the day, by each user, for each row of data. So, assuming we have constructed the correct formula, we might end up with some rows of data that show a usage of 2 min for the day, and another set of rows that show 50 min of usage for the day. HOWEVER, if the formula is based on the day, none of the rows are going to show a usage of 52 min for the day. And this is why a calculated column is said to be static. The formula in each row evaluates that answer in relation to the values in that row. If that row is only looking at frequency for a day, then that is all the formula will return, regardless of how we construct the pivot table at the other end. You can of course filter the result out via the pivot — but you cannot use the pivot to change how the calculated column calculated the value for that row. Consequently, when we run a pivot over the data we need to be aware of this limitation. For example, you will end up with nonsense data if you build a pivot that has minutes' frequency of usage as either a pivot column or row label, if your data includes more than 1 day of usage. If I build a frequency distribution of usage based on minutes users were active for a day, and do not filter down to specific day, then when I counted the number of distinct users for each frequency of usage, I would be counting the individual in this example twice — once for 2 min, and another for 50 min. If you think that is valid, then imagine you are presenting on your data, and someone asks how come the numbers in the rows add up to more than the total. Good luck explaining what this means, and explaining how such double counting does not invalidate your data!

This means we need a calculated column for each period over which we want to measure frequency of usage. I have created two such periods, one based on all the data, and another based on day. If you are building a pivot table that covers all the data, then use the FrequencyMinutesTotal field. If you are building a pivot that only looks at a single day, then use the FrequencyMinutesDay field.

Calculating the frequency of usage is relatively simple. However, I have done this with two calculated columns, even though it could be done with one, to help make these formulas easier to understand. The formula for the first calculated column, "KeyMinutesActive,' is:

=[UserName]&[FormattedDate]

If I wanted to count the number of minutes a user has been actively accessing library resources I cannot simply count the number of rows in the LibraryUsage table. A user might have a dozen entries for the same minute, and another user might have 30 log entries for the same minute. In both cases, however, we only want to know that each user has been active for a minute. So running a straight count on the rows will not help. Furthermore, it will just provide nonsense data, as the number of entries in the ezproxy log is just a function of the resource the user happens to be accessing at the time. You might as well count the number of different colors on a book cover to assess whether it is worth reading.

It is possible to turn the random nature of the log into something meaningful, and in this case it can be achieved by stripping out the seconds in the date-time stamp and combining this data with the username. Given that the seconds have already been stripped out in the formula FormattedDate, this means the only thing that needs to be done to create a combined key is to join the username and the formatted date. Now, if you do a straight count on this new calculated column you will still get nonsense. However, if you count the number of distinct values in the KeyMinutesActive column, you will suddenly get meaningful data! If a user had 30 rows of data for a given minute, then all those 30 rows would have the same value in the column KeyMinutesActive. They would have the user (say "jbloggs," and the formatted date, say "9/02/2015 15:16:00"). If all 30 rows are the same, and we did a distinct count of the values, we would get the answer 1. Another way of thinking about it is imagine we removed all the duplicates in those 30 rows, how many rows of data would we be left with? This answer one is meaningful because it allows us to identify that one user was actively retrieving library resources sometime during the 1 min block that occurred on 9/02/2015 15:16:00. By itself this is not useful, but we now have a method for meaningfully counting data, and that data can then be rolled up at a reporting level to something that is useful.

FrequencyMinutesTotal

Once a combined key for user and time has been created ("KeyMinutesActive"), the next step is to use that key to perform counts. The formula KeyMinutesActive is just a stepping stone to this formula.

The calculated column FrequencyMinutesTotal specifies how many minutes in total a user has been actively accessing library resources over the whole of the data in your cube. The formula for FrequencyMinutesTotal is:

```
=CALCULATE(
    DISTINCTCOUNT(LibraryUsage[KeyMinutesActive]),
    NOT(ISBLANK(LibraryUsage[FormattedDate])),
    ALLEXCEPT(LibraryUsage, LibraryUsage[UserName])
)+0
```

The CALCULATE part of the formula achieves two things. Firstly, it forces the formula to iterate over every row in the LibraryUsage table. This is essential, as I need to know how many blocks of minutes' library resources were being used for. If this was the only information I needed, I could have just used a distinct count on the column "KeyMinutesActive." However, I need to know how many blocks of minutes the library user in the current row has tallied up. This is where the second part of the CALCULATE function comes into play, as it can be used to filter results. I need to filter the results to skip the nonuser rows (i.e., those with blank dates), and filter to the user on the current row.

The NOT(ISBLANK(...) function filters out non-library users, and ALLEXCEPT filters to the username in the current row. Alternatively, you could use a combination of the functions "COUNTROWS(SUMMARIZE..." to eliminate the need for the KeyMinutesActive calculated column.

KeyYearMonthDay

The KeyYearMonthDay formula has the same purpose as the KeyMinutesActive Formula, except this formula is designed to identify the frequency of usage of library resources by day. The formula is:

```
=LEFT(LibraryUsage[Date], 12)
```

If we want to know the frequency distribution of usage of library resources for a specific day, then we need a way of identifying a specific day as unique. The combined key needs to uniquely identify the day. I can't just use the day, because if the data spans more than a single month, then the day will no longer be unique. There are many ways to build a key that uniquely identifies each individual day, and I did this the simplest way I could think of, just grab the date portion of the date-time string. So this formula grabs the first 12 characters from the Date column.

By itself this formula does nothing; it is only a stepping stone on a path to the next formula.

FrequencyMinutesDay

The FrequencyMinutesDay formula is used to identify for each row, the frequency of usage for the day for the user in that row. This calculated column can be used in a pivot table to show the frequency of usage for a given day. The formula is:

```
=CALCULATE(
  DISTINCTCOUNT(LibraryUsage[KeyMinutesActive]),
    NOT(ISBLANK(LibraryUsage[FormattedDate])),
    ALLEXCEPT(LibraryUsage,LibraryUsage[USERNAME],LibraryUsage
    [KeyYearMonthDay])
  )+0
```

This formula is similar to FrequencyMinutesTotal. The ALLEXCEPT section limits the distinct count to rows that have the same username and KeyYearMonthDay value as the current row. ALLEXCEPT only takes base tables as arguments. So if you are up for a challenge, eliminating the need for KeyYearMonthDay will require a very different formula.

Location

The purpose of the location formula is to identify where the user was located when they accessed the resource, by looking at the IP address. The formula is:

```
=IF(ISBLANK(LibraryUsage[FormattedDate]), BLANK(),
   IF(related(LocationTable[Student location])=BLANK(), "Off campus",
      RELATED(LocationTable[Student location])
   )
)
```

There are two nested IF statements in this formula. The first level checks whether the FormattedDate is blank, and if it is blank, then return a blank value, and stop there. Remember, the LibraryUsage table contains nonusers. If a student had not used a library resource, then they will not have any IP address to report on. Therefore, if they are a nonuser, then we don't want any value to be returned in the Location field. If the FormattedDate is not blank, then the second nested IF statement comes into play. The second IF statement checks whether the IP address exists in the LocationTable. If it does not exist, then it will return "Off campus," and stop there. If the IP address does exist in the LocationTable, then the RELATED formula will go and fetch the "Student Location" for that IP address from the LocationTable.

NOTE: This formula will return an error until a relationship is created between the LibraryUsage table and the LocationTable. Do not worry; the error will disappear once the relationship is created.

GroupMinutesDay

This formula groups library users' minutes spent accessing resources into frequency bins:

```
=LOOKUPVALUE(FreqMinutesTable[FreqMinutesDescription],FreqMinutesTable
[Start],
   CALCULATE(MAX(FreqMinutesTable[Start]),
      FILTER(FreqMinutesTable,
         FreqMinutesTable[start]<=LibraryUsage[FrequencyMinutesDay] &&
         FreqMinutesTable[stop]>=LibraryUsage[FrequencyMinutesDay]
      )
   )
)
```

This formula is looking in the FreqMinutesTable for a row where the frequency of usage in the current row for the LibraryUsage table is between the frequency stop and start time in the FreqMinutesTable. When it finds that row, it returns the FreqMinutesDescription value. This is only a little bit more complicated than the usual vanilla flavored VLOOKUP in normal Excel. The CALCULATE part of the formula forces Excel to iterate over every row of the FreqMinutesDayTable, which is necessary, as there is no relationship between the FreqMinutesTable, and the LibraryUsage table.

GroupMinutesTotal

This formula is almost identical to GroupMinutesDay. The only change is that the FrequencyMinutesDay is substituted with FrequencyMinutesTotal:

```
=LOOKUPVALUE(FreqMinutesTable[FreqMinutesDescription],FreqMinutesTable
[Start],
    CALCULATE(MAX(FreqMinutesTable[Start]),
      FILTER(FreqMinutesTable,
        FreqMinutesTable[start]<=LibraryUsage[FrequencyMinutesTotal] &&
        FreqMinutesTable[stop]>=LibraryUsage[FrequencyMinutesTotal]
              )
        )
  )
```

Creating relationships

As explained in the previous chapter, you can use PowerPivot to create one-to-many relationships. You can also use PowerPivot to create many-to-many relationships, but these are far too complex for this book, and with clever Fact Table construction, for the most part you should be able to avoid the need to create M2M relationships. Creating a relationship between two tables will make it much easier to write formulas that span across tables, and it will improve what you can do with your pivot tables.

There are two relationships you will need to create, one joining the DateTable to the LibraryUsage table, and the other joining the LocationTable to the LibraryUsage table.

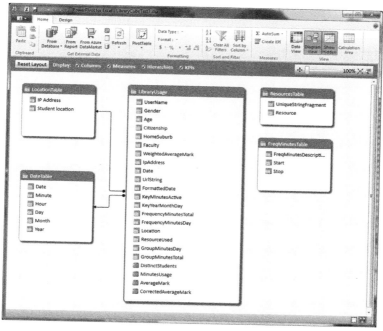

Linking the location table is very easy. Open the PowerPivot window, and click on the "Diagram View" icon. Next click on the IP address column from either the LibraryUsage or LocationTable, and drag it across to the IP address column on the other table. Just like magic, a relationship is created. For this join to work, you cannot have duplicate values in the IP Address column in the LocationTable. The LibraryUsage table will have many duplicate IP addresses, and PowerPivot can only link two tables if one of the tables does not have duplicates. In other words, PowerPivot can only create a one-to-many relationship between two tables.

Linking the DateTable to the LibraryUsage table is a little bit more involved. You need to ensure that the data type for the dates in both tables match. If, for example, the "FormattedDate" column in the LibraryUsage table is defined as text, then you will not be able to link it to the date table, which should be defined as a date data type. If you do not define your date data types correctly, then your date sensitive formulas will not work. To format the data type in PowerPivot, click on the "DataView" icon, then select the LibraryUsage table, and click on the FormattedDate column. The Date Type Menu is located in the middle of the Home menu. You should pick a custom Date format that matches the date format you used in your DateTable.

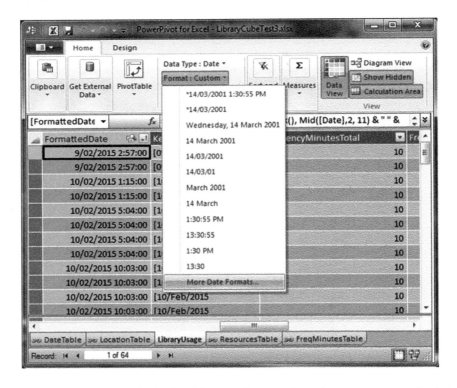

Once the date fields in both tables are formatted to date, you can go back to the Diagram View, and drag the Date column from your DateTable, over the top of the FormattedDate column in your LibraryUsage table. Remember, you cannot join against the Date column in the LibraryUsage table, as that data is not a date — it has the stray "[" character at the start of the text. Don't worry if you did this, I forgot about this, and could not work out why I could not get the two "Date" columns to join! It took me 10 min to work out what I was doing wrong!

Writing measures

To create measures, first of all you need to create a PivotTable from the PowerPivot model. You can do this two ways, via the PowerPivot window, or via the PowerPivot Menu on the normal Excel page. After you have added a PowerPivot PivotTable, you will see something like this:

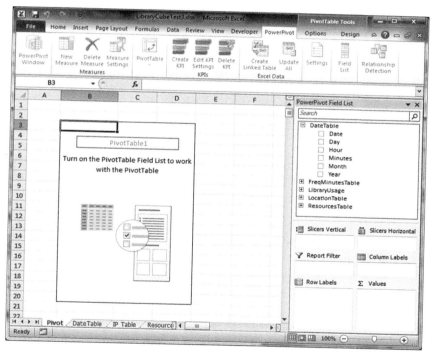

I have expanded out the DateTable, so you can see all the other tables in this screenshot. You can add measures to any of these tables, but there is only one that will make sense to add measures to, and that is the main table, "LibraryUsage." Remember, to add the measure you can right click over the LibraryUsage table, and select "Add New Measure."

DistinctStudents

This measure will count the number of unique students.

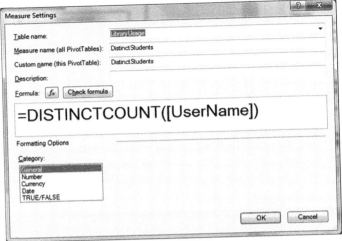

No matter how many times Jane Smith appears in the data, she will only be counted once in a pivot cell, and the totals will only count her once. If one person can be in many categories, then there may be some overlap. For example, if Jane Smith belonged to two faculties, and you used Faculty as a column or row label, then she will be counted once under both Faculties. However, she will only be counted once in the total, which means the rows will add up to more than the total. However, this is precisely the behavior we need from this measure, and if you explain to your audience that some students can belong to many faculties, then they should understand why the total for all the faculties is less than the sum of the individual faculties.

MinutesActive

This measure counts the number of 1 min blocks in which a student was actively retrieving library resources.

The formula is:

```
=CALCULATE (
  COUNTROWS (
    SUMMARIZE (
      LibraryUsage,
      LibraryUsage[FormattedDate],
      LibraryUsage[UserName]
    )
  ),
  NOT ( ISBLANK ( LibraryUsage[Date] ) )
)
```

Remember, the LibraryUsage table may contain several rows of data for the same period of access. This is a function of the log. Also, some students may have many rows of data in your "StudentData" table. For example, if you asked for students' faculty to be included in the student data you requested, then you will almost certainly have more than one row of data for some students. SUMMARISE returns a table that removes all the duplicate combinations of UserName and FormattedDate. The last part of the formula filters out non-users.

AverageMark

If you wish to correlate library usage with student marks, then you should collect a single weighted average mark at the end of the semester. Obviously, do not try to correlate library usage to marks that were obtained prior to the library usage, or more than a semester past the library usage. Your sample size will be critical here, as will be the times you collect the samples. Do not expect to find a simple correlation between marks and library usage, the factors influencing academic performance are far too complex to reduce them down to a simple mechanistic relationship. And on this point, you simply will not have access to the broad range of other variables contributing to academic performance, so you will have no defensible way of controlling for these variables. However, you are not writing a scientific paper, you simply want to know that students who use your resources are not worse off, and on the face of things there is some evidence to support the argument that you are helping their performance.

The formula for the AverageMark measure is:

```
=AVERAGEX(
    DISTINCT(LibraryUsage[UserName]),
    CALCULATE(
        AVERAGE(LibraryUsage[WeightedAverageMark])
    )
)
```

AVERAGEX iterates over every row in the table. I am only interested in averaging the marks of distinct students. In other words, if because of the random nature of the ezproxy log, Jane appears in the log 100 times for a given 1 min block, and Joe only once, then I do not want to take the average of 100 times Jane's mark, plus one instance of Joe's mark, divided by 101. That would just give me nonsense data. If the maths behind this is not clear for you, then consider this, the more rows of data there are in the LibraryUsage table for a given student, the more weighting their mark would receive. We don't want this. The solution is to only look at the average mark for distinct students. Hence the first part of the formula. The next part of the formula, the CALCULATE function, also iterates over every row in the table. This time, however, it is just taking the average for the user in the current row context.

This formula will work even if your student table includes, say for example, different marks the student obtained for each faculty. This is because due to the way I have suggested the ezproxy logs be joined to the student data, each student should have an equal number of rows in the LibraryUsageTable for each faculty that the student belongs to. If this is not the case, you will need to use the AverageMark measure as a stepping stone to an average mark measure that correctly rolls up the rows. This might be something like this:

=AVERAGEX(SUMMARIZE(LibraryUsage, LibraryUsage[UserName], LibraryUsage[Faculty]), LibraryUsage[AverageMark])

You will need to test and adjust this measure to suit your dataset.

Some suggested views

Here are a few suggested views. Remember that I have populated the datasets with random data, so there will be no patterns, the actual numbers you see here are meaningless. Hopefully, when you plug your data into the cube, you will see some patterns of data that you can act upon.

Minutes of usage by resource accessed and faculty

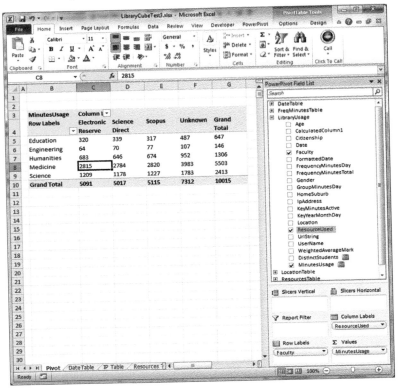

Since the time is being counted at such a granular level, it is reasonable to say that if a student has been active during a 1 min block of time, they have been actively retrieving resources for 1 min. A student may have in fact only spent 10 s accessing a resource, but still be counted as having accessed resources for a minute. This is not an issue, however, as most students will have accessed resources for more than a single 1 min block. It's hard to imagine that there will be enough instances of students accessing resources for less than 1 min to have a meaningful impact on the data. Nevertheless, the time actually spent accessing resources will be lower than that recorded in this table. You just need to explain the methodology to your audience, even if it is just in a footnote to a table.

Frequency distribution of student usage of resources by faculty

This view shows the distribution of usage by faculty. For example, there were 17 unique students from the Education Faculty that never accessed library resources during the sample period. You can easily convert these figures to percentages by right clicking on the pivot table, then click "Show Values As">"% of Column Total." This will give you the proportion of nonusers by Faculty, as well as the distribution across the frequency of usage. This view uses FrequencyMinutesTotal as the row label; if you wanted to use FrequencyMinutesDay, remember to filter your results to a specific day, otherwise your data will be nonsense. You could also use the higher level frequency groupings, to reduce the number of rows by aggregating the data to broader frequency "bins."

Frequency minutes usage	Education	Engineering	Humanities	Medicine	Science	Grand Total
0	17	19		36	27	98
1				3		3
2	1		1	2		4
3	1		2	8	4	15
4	1		3	17	10	31
5	1	1	8	16	16	42
6	11		2	32	17	62
7	9	4	12	39	22	86
8	2	1	13	58	34	108
9	4	2	17	47	23	93
10	8		12	63	24	107
11	4	3	16	54	19	96
12	3	1	9	50	19	82
13	3		8	39	18	68
14	4	3	6	23	14	50
15	3		6	24	9	42
16	6		4	16	4	30
17			3	17	4	24
18	1		3	11	5	20
19	2			2		4
20			1	3	2	6
21				1	2	3
22			1	1		2
23				1		1
26				2		2
Grand Total	81	34	127	565	273	1079

Frequency usage by hours

You can create this chart by dragging the Day and Hour from the DateTable onto either your column or row labels, then dragging DistinctStudents into the Values Box.

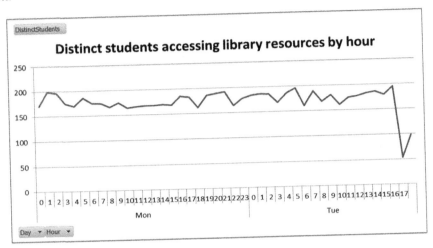

You could also do the same for MinutesUsage. These types of charts will give you an idea of the variation in usage, which should be useful for scheduling support, and for measuring the success of promotions aimed at improving usage of library resources.

Average mark by frequency of library usage

This view shows the average marks students obtained by frequency of usage of library resources (in minutes), and home suburb. Once again, the data here is random, so there are no patterns.

Home suburb	Zero usage	1 to 15 minutes	16 to 30 minutes	Average
Arbutus	59.0	70.4	70.3	69.7
Baltimore Highlands	50.0	72.4	76.0	70.9
Bethlehem	55.8	71.3	54.0	69.0
Brooklyn Park	36.7	67.7	70.3	65.1
Carney	53.0	69.3	100.0	69.2
Catonsville	50.3	74.8	58.0	72.2
Colonie	39.5	71.3	70.0	69.4
Delmar	44.0	66.6	76.8	65.3
Dundalk	63.7	72.9	60.0	71.0
East Greenbush	48.0	68.9		66.3
Guilderland	52.0	66.5	70.3	65.7
Halethorpe	56.5	66.3	69.8	65.7
Lansdowne	55.5	75.3	65.4	71.0
Linthicum	44.3	70.5	66.0	67.8
Lochearn	53.8	71.1	83.7	70.2
Menands	49.7	71.5	72.0	70.1
North Greenbush	60.7	65.3	56.0	64.4
Overlea	49.3	70.9	72.7	68.5
Parkville	57.3	65.9	96.0	65.7
Pikesville	44.0	69.4	54.0	67.3
Pumphrey	51.5	69.9	84.0	68.1
Rensselaer	43.3	71.9	81.2	71.1
Riderwood	63.3	72.0	71.0	71.0
Rodgers Forge	60.3	71.7	72.7	71.0
Rosedale	53.6	70.5	64.3	68.6
Ruxton	44.2	71.5	78.3	68.1
Slingerlands	37.0	73.1	56.5	70.9
Sudbrook Park	56.5	75.7	86.5	72.7
Towson	56.5	67.8	70.5	67.4
Woodlawn	54.5	72.2	67.0	70.9
Grand Total	**52.1**	**70.5**	**70.8**	**68.9**

There are of course many other views you could create. You could also create other calculated columns and measures. The information I have provided will help you to set up a basic desktop library cube, based on samples of your electronic resource usage logs. Once you have developed your PowerPivot skills, you will be able to expand on this cube, and perhaps use PowerPivot to provide intelligence on other datasets.

Beyond the ordinary

I was in East Germany (DDR) when the Berlin wall came down. The background to this story is too detailed and irrelevant to go into here. What is relevant about this story is how quickly things unraveled in the DDR. Before 1989, there were many problems, but everything still had the appearance of being solid. Those people that had a grip on power, appeared to have a firm grip, and even though there was dissent, change did not seem imminent. Those in power in the DDR concentrated all their efforts on maintaining the status quo, and the focus was on looking good, rather than being good. So, as the difference between the east and the west widened, and the propaganda in the east looked thinner and thinner, there was little substance in the DDR to hold things together when the Soviet Union changed direction, and internal dissent began to grow. So, like a house of cards, something that looked solid from the outside collapsed with such speed that it left you wondering how it had survived so long.

Many people imagine when they grab numbers, all emotion goes out the window, and the act of grabbing at numbers makes things objective, scientific. Well, it does not. Many people see what they want to see, and use numbers to justify this. I used to dabble in the stock market, and would occasionally lurk in the odd stock chat room. You would think with shares that it would all be about numbers. You would think people would look at things such as the price-to-earnings ratio, the cash flow, the assets, their market share, the potential growth and so forth. You would think that these things are objective facts, putting aside the odd cooked book, and that share purchase and sale decisions would be guided by these objective facts. But they are not. I have observed many people ride a stock down to nothing, becoming euphoric with each fleeting uptrend, and acting as cheerleaders as they rode the rollercoaster down to its inevitable bottom. No one can question their decision to hang onto that stock even in the face of overwhelming evidence. Anyone who questions the stock is booed off stage.

The fact is, buying shares is not a financial decision for many people, it is an emotional one. If they sell the share they are admitting that they made a wrong decision, and so many people's egos are either too fragile, or so big, that they cannot accept the possibility that they made a mistake. Yet, to get rich on the stock market, and do this through skill rather than luck, you need to be dispassionate. You need to recognize that you will make bad decisions at times, recognize when you have done this, and change tack accordingly. But you cannot do this if you spend your whole time only collecting data that makes your share purchase decisions look good. If you focus on looking good, you will eventually lose all your money on the stock market, unless you have lucked on the right shares. If on the other hand you focus on being good, and collect data that can help you to be good, then you will have a fighting chance of success. Moreover, if you do succeed, you will automatically look good too. However, if you find yourself in that situation, looking good may no longer be so important.

In East Germany in 1989, the new people in power seemed to make a few last desperate efforts to focus on being good, rather than just looking good. But it is no good trying to change at one second to midnight, when all the forces that will bring about your demise are on an inescapable collision course. They left it all too late.

The library sector too is under threat, and everything that seems solid now can vanish in the blink of a historical eye. Libraries have centuries of history, and for centuries have played a critical role in distributing knowledge. This history does not guarantee a future. And, if you don't focus your efforts on being good, but instead on looking good, then your library risks drifting faster toward hostile external changes; and in the process your library will forfeit influence for reaction.

If you want to be successful in the share market, you have to be dispassionate, you have to see things as they really are, and act accordingly. If you want to be successful in business you have to do the same. The feedback mechanisms for the library sector are slower than the share market. If you make a poor share purchase decision, the market will soon let you know. The flow of feedback in the public policy area is much slower, and more complicated. But it still flows. The lack of a rapid feedback mechanism does not mean you are insulated from change, it just means you have more time for more decisions. This economic feedback delay provides a buffer, and this buffer is a gift. If you are to use this buffer wisely, it will be to focus on how you can make your library be good.

To answer that question, how can I focus on being good, you have to come back to the core question: what value are we actually providing? There is no point attempting to collect any data aimed at being good, if you cannot succinctly and concretely describe your value proposition. Once you know what your value proposition actually is, and you can describe it in concrete words that actually mean something real; only then can you do things such as: measure how well you deliver against that value proposition; improve the efficiency with which you deliver that value proposition; and improve that value proposition itself. I think this is something that many library managers will struggle with in this changing world, and it is ultimately the reason why, when they are honest with themselves in the moments outside of the political spotlight, that they might be displeased with their performance and operational data.

I cannot tell you what your value proposition is; this is something you need to sort out for yourself. However, I can tell you that if you do develop a clear, sustainable and compelling value proposition for your services, then you are on the path to doing something beyond the ordinary with your data.

For example, if your key value proposition is to develop active communities of readers, then your focus will be on building, sustaining and growing social groups that are focused on reading. Your measures, therefore, might include more than just counts of participation; they might include qualitative data — such as stories about how these groups have changed individuals' lives. You can use this data then, to focus on where you are getting the greatest impact, and replicating these success drivers across the program. You can also use this data to grow the program, as most people connect with stories, rather than numbers. But in doing all this, the question you always need to keep asking yourself, is how is our program providing something unique, where is this program succeeding, and where is the value added too thin to be sustainable. In other words, you need to be critical, not just cherry pick the good stories to use as marketing fodder for stakeholders and clients. To do this you will need numbers to keep you objective. The basic counts of participation will allow you to critically contextualize the qualitative feedback. If you have fantastic feedback, but when you drill into the participation you find that most of your social reading activities have fewer than three participants, then you will know that something is wrong, and you will not take the good news stories at face value. You can also use some more sophisticated quantitative data to assess the validity of the qualitative data. For example, your programs should build social networks. You could measure participant's exposure to new social networks by mapping their movement through the different groups and programs you are supporting. If you find that it is mostly the same group of people attending most of your programs, then once again you will know something is not working, and that you need to look at the root cause of why the program is not attracting new people.

If you want to be good, you need data to inform critical thinking, and you need to listen dispassionately and act on any criticism the data is providing. This is why using data to be good is so much more difficult than using data to simply look good. If you only use data to look good, then you can just cherry pick the good stories. However, if you do this, and your program is only attracting a small cohort of faithful followers, then how long do you think such a program will be able to stand up against external scrutiny when funding becomes a critical issue, and the library is one of the biggest line items in your organization's budget?

If you are still struggling with how data could be used to do more than the ordinary, consider the following. When it comes to teaching information literacy, or whatever the terminology for that area of learning is used, then the typical approach of most academic libraries I have seen is to count the number of classes, count the length of the class, and count the number of participants. Staff might also count the amount of time they spent on preparation, and they might provide more detailed data on the attendees, such as whether they were first year students, etc. Finally, they might ask for feedback via a survey. If you look at the data through the lens of what you currently do, rather than through the lens of what is possible, you will end up with "so what" data that at best only tells you how busy you are. So what is possible? This of course will vary from one library to the next. At the most basic level, it is possible to improve the academic skills of many more students than you currently teach. So, if this is your target, then at the very least you need to know what proportion of the cohort you are reaching, and how successful your targeted efforts have been. To achieve this you might integrate marketing with information literacy. Marketing needs data to have a reasonable chance of success. So you will need to know which students are attending (i.e., collect their student numbers), which students are not attending (i.e., any student number you have not collected), and then actually use this data. You would use the data to assess your current market share, to analyze variability, and identify any patterns of behavior that need to be taken into consideration. For example, are some staff consistently more successful than others at attracting student audiences, do some student cohorts have a greater proportion of attendees than others, does the time, day, and period in the semester have a significant influence on attendance, etc.? You would then use that information to target specific audiences with promotions, but you would not stop there. You would understand the level of variability in attendance, and you would identify a quantum that lies outside that level of variation as a clear indicator that the promotion had succeeded, and that any change that did occur was not just a random by product of the normal level of attendance variation for your current system. You would use the data you have collected on post promotion attendance to assess the promotion's success, and you would all come together as a group to brainstorm the potential root causes for a promotion's success or failure. You would then refine your promotions, and try again. You would always have measures in place to be able to determine whether something was successful, and in making that determination you would have a sound understanding of the normal variation in your data. There are many more things you could do with such an approach, but you should get the idea by now.

Whatever data you use to improve your performance and impact, the path to success is to take a more scientific approach to the use of data. What a lot of library data does at the moment is tell a "so what" story. This is not good enough, and you do not have to settle for this.

Note: Screenshots of Microsoft Excel, Microsoft Access and Microsoft Notepad containing material in which Microsoft retains copyright have been used with permission from Microsoft.

Index

Printed and bound by CPI Group (UK) Ltd, Croydon, CR0 4YY

08/06/2025

01896874-0004